D1616980

HALL OF MIRRORS

FRANCE
SPRING 1942

London

Dunkerque

Military administration of Belgium and Northern France

Dieppe

Coastal military zone ("Atlantic Wall") entry prohibited

GLORIA

INTERALLIED (PARIS)

AUTOGIRO

Paris

Nez Rouge

OCCUPIED FRANCE
German military occupation

DEMARCATION LINE

Cosne

SWITZERLAND

Atlantic Ocean

Creuse

Vichy

Lyon

HECKLER

Haute Loire

ALPS

ITALY

Mauzac

Bergerac

Bordeaux

VENTRILOQUIST

Le Puy

UNOCCUPIED ZONE

Toulouse

Marseille

URCHIN

Nice

Pyrenees Mountains

Perpignan

San Juan de las Abadesas

Figueras

Mediterranean Sea

SPAIN

Barcelona

Madrid

HALL *of* MIRRORS

VIRGINIA HALL: AMERICA'S GREATEST SPY OF WWII

CRAIG GRALLEY

Chrysalis

Publisher's Cataloging-in-Publication Data
Names: Gralley, Craig R.
Title: Hall of mirrors : Virginia Hall, America's greatest spy of World War II / Craig Gralley.
Description: Pisgah Forest, NC : Chrysalis Books, 2019.| Includes
    1 map. | Summary: Breaking through barriers of physical lim-
    itation and gender discrimination, Virginia Hall enters France
    during the Nazi occupation and becomes America's greatest
    spy of World War II.
Identifiers: LCCN 2018915102 | ISBN 9781733541503 (hardback) |
    ISBN 9781733541534 (pbk.) | ISBN 9781733541510 (EPUB)
    | ISBN 9781733541527 (MOBI)
Subjects: LCSH: Goillot, Virginia, 1906-1982 -- Fiction. | Women
spies -- United States -- Fiction. |
    | World War, 1939-1945 -- Underground movements – France
    -- Fiction. | People with disabilities -- Fiction.| BISAC:
    FICTION / Historical / World War II. | FICTION / War &
    Military.
Classification: LCC PS3607.R35 H35 2019| DDC 813 G73--dc22
LC record available at https://lccn.loc.gov/2018915102

First Edition

Book Design by Glen M.Edelstein, Hudson Valley Book Design

For Janet and Will for your sustaining love.

For Virginia and all the silent heroes of OSS and CIA, who risked their lives for freedom.

FOREWORD AND ACKNOWLEDGMENTS

Few Americans know our country's first and greatest spy of the Second World War was a disabled woman from Baltimore named Virginia Hall.

Recruited by British Intelligence at a time when the US had not yet entered the war, Virginia became the Allies' first agent to live and spy on the Nazis behind the lines in Vichy France. She was an elusive spy, constantly changing names and safe houses to avoid capture by the gestapo. But in the winter of 1942, her luck ran out. Wanted posters appeared demanding capture of "the most dangerous Allied agent," and a bounty was placed on her head. As Gestapo chief Klaus Barbie closed in, Virginia made a harrowing escape across the snow-capped Pyrenees, dragging her prosthetic limb, "Cuthbert," behind her. But Virginia's story didn't end with her escape to Spain. She demanded to return to France to continue the fight. Her British spymasters refused, telling Virginia she was too well known and Klaus Barbie, "the Butcher of Lyon," was still hunting her. But Virginia ignored the dangers—certain capture, horrible torture, a painful death—and returned to France with the new American spy organization, the OSS, on the eve of the D-Day invasion.

Virginia Hall received some of the highest awards British and American military commanders could bestow, but citations and accolades don't tell the larger story of her immense personal courage: how she broke through the barriers of physical limitation and gender discrimination to become America's greatest spy of World War II.

She was an elusive subject who once remarked, "Too many of my friends were killed because they talked too much." It's a criticism that couldn't be directed at Virginia. While many lesser spies wrote freely about their exploits, Virginia Hall remained true to her oath of secrecy long after she retired from her life of espionage. She left no memoirs, granted no interviews, and spoke little about her life overseas—even to her closest friends and relatives. She died in 1982.

Like all spies, Virginia didn't want to be unmasked, even in death, and she only revealed herself to me over the course of a four-year search. Her secrets were like tiles, which I pieced together to form the mosaic of her clandestine life. I found her individual acts of courage in declassified documents held by my former employer, the CIA, and in the US National and British Archives; as a line or two in memoirs written by other World War II spies; as reflections in interviews with CIA historians, a psychiatrist specializing in physical trauma; and with Virginia's last relative who remembered her. But mostly, Virginia revealed herself in the setting she loved most: the field—the cities, towns, and rugged mountains of France, where I discovered the rocky trail she took to freedom in Spain. I found her as well in the world's war-torn areas, where I saw Virginia in the courage and confidence of today's bright women agents.

Hall of Mirrors is based on years of research and hundreds of historical documents but because it is written with dialogue, as Virginia would tell her own story, this is a historical novel. I chose to write it in Virginia's voice because the perspective offers insight into her personal struggles, which forged her resilience and character. For the pure historians among us, the epilogue is written without dialogue and continues the story of Virginia and her agents after the conclusion of the Second World War.

This novel took root in my Master's thesis and was nurtured by teachers and colleagues at the Johns Hopkins University. One of my great Hopkins teachers, author Tim Wendel, challenged me to search for Virginia's Freedom Trail in France and, most generously, provided encouragement and his perspective on publication years after I'd taken my last class. I'm grateful to Mark Farrington, my thesis advisor and the current director of the Writing Program at Hopkins, for his enthusiastic support and key insights on how to improve my draft. In the university's fiction workshop led by Margaret Meyers, women colleagues offered constructive criticism and advice on how to portray a woman's perspective. I'm indebted to Margaret Meyers, Chelsea Newman, Jane Taylor, and Raima Larter for their guidance and counsel. I also thank Debbi Thomas, Lou Mehrer, and Jean Gralley (my successful author/illustrator sister) for their perceptive comments on early drafts. Dr. Larry Pastor, a psychiatrist specializing in trauma, provided valuable insight into the emotional and physical challenges an amputation presents and told me how Virginia's disability, rather than an impediment, awakened a resilience important to her success. Two friends, Frank Jones and Richard Norris, though no longer with us, were early enthusiastic readers. Other friends and colleagues at CIA—particularly, Peter Earnest, Founding Executive Director of the International Spy Museum in Washington—offered their expertise on topics ranging from espionage tradecraft to book publication. I'd also like to thank the women of CIA, who collectively demonstrate why our country has the best intelligence service in the world.

The employees at the British archive, Kew, and William Cunliffe of the National Archives in College Park, MD, provided expert assistance as did CIA historian and former museum curator, Toni Hiley. Lorna Catling, Virginia Hall's niece and keeper of the flame was very generous in sharing her time and memories of Aunt Virginia. Thank you.

I'm most grateful to those established authors who understood the unique challenges of being a first-time novelist and extended themselves to offer encouragement and advice. Fellow CIA authors and successful spy novelists Jason Matthews and Mark Henshaw, Pulitzer Prize winning author David E. Hoffman, and my former Great Falls neighbors—biographer Walter Stahr, and author and freelance journalist, Kristin Clark Taylor—all taught me important lessons in generosity. I enjoyed my semi-regular give-and-take with British author Sonia Purnell, who is completing her own book, a biography of Virginia Hall titled *A Woman of No Importance*. I appreciated her perceptive comments on my writing, too, and wish her much success. We share the conviction that Virginia's story needs to be told. I'd also like to thank Glen Edelstein of Hudson Valley Book Design; Illustrator, Michael Gellatly; Web Designer, Kristin McCurry; Photographer, Luanne Allgood; and Lana Allen and Ralph Henley of JKS Communications for their help in readying *Hall of Mirrors* and making it available to a wider audience.

All successful authors know it's impossible to create anything of value without the love and support of those closest to you. My wife, Janet, and son, Will, were the ones who bore the brunt of my isolation, and I can't thank them enough for their patience and enduring love.

Craig Gralley
Great Falls, Virginia
February 2019
www.craiggralley.com

I would give anything to get my hands on that limping bitch.

KLAUS BARBIE
GESTAPO CHIEF, LYON

HALL OF MIRRORS

NOVEMBER 1942. Snow was falling in the Pyrenees.

The port of Marseilles was filling with Nazis soldiers fleeing the Allies' assault on North Africa. The borders to France were closing, and the secret police had broken through my door on Rue Groll in Lyon. But I'd vanished hours earlier on the last train to Perpignan and had begun my climb up the rugged mountains to Spain, my wooden leg, Cuthbert, dragging a path through the snow behind me.

I'd stayed hidden for so long. I was a ghost without a name. The gestapo called me the Greek goddess, Artemis; wanted posters with only a sketch labeled me, "the most dangerous Allied agent." To the French Resistance, the "maquis," I was La Dame Qui Boite— "the lady who limps," and Klaus Barbie, the Nazi butcher hunting me, had his own name. I was "the limping bitch".

London was right. To stay alive, I had to become a phantom, even to my own agents. My spymasters called me a number, Agent 3844, and sent me off to war with forged documents bearing the names Marie Monin, Brigitte LeContre, Marcelle Montagne, and Ana Muller. They said I should remain a mystery and say nothing about my real life. So behind enemy lines, I became Germaine, Philomene, Marie, Diane, Nicolas, or Camille.

Even back home when I was growing up, my family called me Dindy. But my true name is Virginia Hall.

CHAPTER ONE

Miss Virginia Hall who works at the US embassy talked at my house last night. It strikes me that this lady, a native of Baltimore, might well be used for a mission . . .

MAURICE BUCKMASTER
SPECIAL OPERATIONS EXECUTIVE
LONDON, 15 JANUARY 1941

My memory has become a shadow to me now, but I remember being in Paris the day it fell to the Nazis. I was shaken, as I suppose everyone was, by how quickly and brutally the end came. The air was thick with terror and dread as Parisians, desperate to escape the advancing German army, choked the streets, leaving the capital with every conveyance imaginable—automobiles, bicycles, horse-drawn carts piled high with life's possessions. Adding to the panic, overhead the German Luftwaffe was firing on the fleeing masses, strafing the innocent without pity or discrimination. I was part of that horrible exodus.

People forget how dire it was for all of Europe. Britain, just across the channel, was France's best hope, but London itself was a smoking ruin. The battle for Britain was being fought in the skies, and our own diplomats back in Washington thought the island country was lost. Churchill was right when he said the world was on a narrow ledge overlooking the abyss of a new dark age.

It was their blackest hour, but somehow I knew London was where I was meant to be. So I made my way across Spain to the coast of Portugal and told the British consular official in Lisbon that I had been an ambulance driver in France. Maybe that's why he let me in.

JANUARY 1941, ENGLAND

One winter day, a most unusual woman approached me in Grosvenor Square, where I worked as a code clerk for the US War Department. She introduced herself as Delphine and mentioned casually that we had a mutual friend at the US embassy, David Bruce with the Red Cross. Delphine was a handsome brunette with narrow red lips and a smoky voice, full of poise and self-assurance. She spoke of Bruce in a precise and perceptive way, spicing her irreverent language with wry humor and a dash of salt. Still, what I remember most about my new acquaintance were her eyes, how penetrating they were. Like little black magnets that tracked my own. It was a most peculiar habit, her observing me. Not personal, but icy, professional.

I rather enjoy uncovering the hidden stories of strangers, so of course I said yes when this mysterious woman asked me to dinner on Baker Street, the same neighborhood of Doyle's Sherlock Holmes. Precisely at seven p.m. the butler, Park, opened the door and Delphine was by his side. This time Delphine, in an evening dress with a red rose pinned to her breast, introduced herself as Vera— Vera Atkins. She didn't respond to the puzzled look on my face. She took my hand and led me across the threshold and into her world. Clothed in a black silk cocktail dress with a single strand of Mikimoto pearls, I was shown to the study where an Army officer was waiting. Major Buckmaster, a tall, thin, bookish man, greeted me in French, then extended his hand. Strange how the evening progressed. Miss Atkins and Major Buckmaster already knew much about me: where I had gone to school, the courses I had taken, the languages I spoke. Dinner was a comfortable affair, fortified by several bottles of good Bordeaux, and both Miss Atkins and Major Buckmaster seemed keenly interested in my escape from France. The dinner conversation continued in the hunt room—a dark paneled space full of stuffed animals and trophy heads. Our talk drifted easily between French and English. We drank cognac and smoked Gauloise Bleu.

Swirling the amber liquid in his snifter, Major Buckmaster turned quiet, then finally opened the door to his secret world.

"You know," he said, "we're in the cooker now. Chamberlain, the bastard, believed Hitler's word in Munich, a ball's up move if there ever was one. Well then, Bob's your uncle and what's done is done. Now it's our job to clean up this bloody mess." His eyes narrowed and his forehead became furrowed. "Eventually, we'll need to take the fight to the Jerrys. Play on their pitch and push them back. Reclaim France for the French. That sort of thing. But we don't have the lads on the ground to tell us what's going on—what the German military mind is thinking, how strongly committed the Frenchies are to resisting. It all hinges on people, people we can trust."

His glass down, the contents spinning slightly, Buckmaster pushed back from the table and locked his hands behind his head.

"When the time is right, as the new PM says, we'll 'set Europe ablaze' with saboteurs. That's my job, and I can't cock it up." Buckmaster said he was the head of a new secret espionage organization within the SOE—the British Special Operations Executive—responsible for placing agents behind German lines in France.

The Major turned quiet and seemed to be studying my reaction. I leaned back, not wanting to appear too eager to know more. My background in acting helped me to present myself as detached. A touch indifferent. But it was a difficult role, because my heart was pounding so hard I was sure they could hear it.

I lifted the glass of wine to my lips and said just before taking that last sip, "And how might I fit into your plans?"

"I was hoping you'd ask," Buckmaster said. "This is all very hush-hush, but you have a security clearance with the Yanks, so you know what I am about to tell you cannot leave this room.

"In the past few months, we trained a handful of British agents, and we've been sprinkling them onto French soil like jimmies on a fairy cake, but we have nothing to show for it. Yes, we can move our spies in and out, but we have no permanent British presence, no bloody foothold in the country. It's the small things that keep tripping us up. If you don't look like you belong, you get picked up by the French secret police and handed over to the gestapo. Wear the wrong kinds of clothing made outside of France. Smoke the wrong brand of cigarettes. Ask for butter for your bread when butter hasn't been seen for weeks. Have a mouth full of nice British fillings instead of the crude gold ones the French have. Ride a bicycle with one hand instead of two. There are a million ways to call attention to yourself. A million ways to get rolled up by the gestapo. If it weren't so damn serious, our performance would be rather laughable, I think. Laughable and pathetic. But now with no information, we've been reduced to relying on Michelin guides to tell us about the country."

Miss Atkins turned her dark, magnetic eyes on me again. "You know France intimately, having lived and gone to school in Paris and Grenoble. You speak French and German fluently. You know the customs and the countryside, so you can move about freely. And you have one big advantage we Brits don't have: that Yankee passport. America's a neutral, so you can travel throughout France. Places where we can't go."

"So," Buckmaster continued, "you ask, 'Why me?' We're in desperate need of people to be our eyes and ears on the ground, to look for landing zones for our Lizzies, to tell us how the French are holding up and take measure of their will to resist, all the while building a network of informants and spies that will allow us, when the time comes, to retake the continent."

Buckmaster looked up from his snifter and into my eyes. His voice slowed and turned low. "I'll give you a couple days to think it over, but before you give me your answer, it's only right that I give you one more bit of news." He hesitated as if searching for words. "It's not hard getting our agents into France, but it's bloody difficult keeping them safe. To be honest, we've been getting knackered. I said we've sent men in, a handful so far and, well, none have reported back."

Miss Atkins added, "We think it's just a matter of time before someone comes to the surface, but we can't know for sure."

"You'll be the first, man or woman, to take up residence behind the lines in Vichy," Buckmaster said. "So here's the whole bloody truth. If the Germans find you're spying, that US passport won't save you. And if the Yanks join the war, then . . . well, your passport will become a liability, and the gestapo will be looking to put your head on their wall like that ibex over there. But we're going to do everything in our power to make sure you stay safe. Give you the same preparation we give our own British agents—weapons, covert communications, all of it, in our training center in Scotland and on our estate near London, Beaulieu." Buckmaster lingered on his next words. "A couple months in Lyon. Eyes and ears. That's all we ask. We know the longer you stay and the more informants you bring under your wing, the more likely you'll draw the attention of the gestapo. And once they find you," he said, groping, "well, let's just say, then the chase is on."

I've been told I inherited my sense of adventure from Grand-father Hall, who at age nine stowed away on a clipper ship. That's why, foolishly perhaps, I completely dismissed Buckmaster's words about "the chase" and how it might end. But most uncharacteristic was how quickly I abandoned my reserve and revealed myself to these two people I'd just met.

"You do know about my leg," I blurted, sliding my chair back and lifting the hem of my black evening dress. Buckmaster didn't look. "And my age," I added.

The Major smiled. "I know all about your relationship with that wooden bloke you call Cuthbert," he said with a boyish half grin. "And your maturity at thirty-five, well, we see that as an advantage. You're experienced. Know how to deal with difficult people and situa-tions." He seemed frustrated. "Look, Virginia, we know all about you, and we wouldn't ask if we didn't think you were up to the job. And I won't kid you. You'd be putting your life in harm's way, facing a grave risk, but it's a manageable risk. We know this isn't America's war, and you don't need to do this."

He paused and became serious, as if he were about to reveal the most vital secret of the evening. "The truth is," he said, "we need you."

Those three short words, offered as a postscript, turned the tumblers that unlocked and opened me completely.

I did give him a day, but the way we talked that evening, we both knew.

I had to say yes.

AUGUST 1941, SPAIN

Buck's words were still rattling around in my head even through the piercing screech of the train's stack. After months of training and then leaving Southampton by freighter just five days ago, I had a gnawing awareness, neither apprehension nor fear but an awakening to the coming danger, and it began to weigh on my chest. Usually when I'm faced with a choice of some consequence, I try to ponder the possibilities, but there always comes a point when I say to hell with it, let's just give it a go. This time I surprised myself by how quickly I agreed to this escapade. But it was an adventure, and I had to be part of it.

Virginia Hall, undercover British spy. At first it seemed a preposterous notion, but then in training, everything seemed so contrived: a fantasy world, an adventure game like the ones I'd played growing up with my brother John back at Box Horn Farm. The truth was that no one—Vera, Buck, the officers, generals, trainers—no one could tell me what it was like to live with the enemy. They prepared me the best they could, but it was all so new. As the first spy to live behind the lines, London wanted me to collect secret information about what was going on inside Vichy, but I also thought myself the canary in a coal mine, showing others who would come later how to survive this hostile new world.

Now having left Lisbon, speeding toward the Nazis in France, I was beginning to see the consequences more clearly. It was if I were on a raft, hurtling down a virgin river strewn with boulders, hearing only the rush of water and not knowing if a thundering Niagara was waiting for me just around the bend.

If pushed, I'd say I was more excited than fearful, comforted by knowing that I was as prepared as anyone could be in the skills of espionage. But still, I was very much alone. Not many Brits could look and play the part of a Frenchman, and the few classmates who joined me in spy school were French nationals sent in for special missions. I'd finished at the top of my class in marksmanship and most of the spy techniques that could be taught.

Vera had boosted my confidence when she took me aside just after an interrogation exercise in Beaulieu and remarked that I had the one skill that all agents must have but could not be taught: the ability to create a believable, spontaneous lie. That requires a quick mind, she said, verbal dexterity, emotional control, and above all, an ability to act extraordinarily ordinary. "That—and having the good sense to keep your eyes and ears open and your mouth shut—is the recipe for staying alive."

My cover story as a reporter for the *New York Evening Post*, provided by a family friend on the paper's board, was the perfect fabrication. It gave me a reason to travel throughout Vichy and ask officials probing questions, prey on their weaknesses and their loyalty to the government, and lure the estranged into my network of spies.

Lying. I suppose it goes against the natural order of things. Some find it hard to keep track of their deceits, what lies were told, when and to whom—all the while not getting caught in a web of their own making. Growing up, I didn't make a habit of lying—my parents made sure of that—but I was a damn good actress at Roland Park Country School. Then in Beaulieu, it occurred to me: on the face of it, spying and acting are the same. It's a masquerade. Convince your mark you're someone you're not. Tell them a story. Sell your character. Above all, become the lie.

My new life would be a full playbill of deceit—almost too many names and characters to keep straight. In my cover job with the *Post*, interviewing officials and for my byline, I'd use my true name, but in recruiting agents, I'd be transformed into Germaine, Philomene, or Marie, changing names as quickly as one might swap an old pair of shoes. If betrayed, the onion could not be peeled back to reveal more than a small circle of conspirators. My life of lies. A hall of mirrors.

The hardest part of training? Mastering London's tools of reporting. Redundancy, they said: for long reports, diagrams, and photographs, send clandestine couriers to the British consulate in Spain or Switzerland. In emergencies, use the diplomatic pouch from a willing neutral embassy. For short messages, rely on Western Union telegrams sent in code to my witting conspirator, my cutout, George Backer at the *New York Post*, who'd forward them to SOE London. And for my most sensitive, top secret communications—to receive approval for agent recruitments and meetings—I'd use my "pianist," a covert radio operator who would make direct contact with my handlers in Bletchley Park outside London.

I admit to being a bit unnerved by the last conversation I had with Buck the evening I departed Southampton. After giving me a money belt filled with 150,000 francs—seed money—Buckmaster's face tightened. "You'll be working solo for a while, that is until your wireless operator surfaces. Albert went missing after being dropped off by our trawler, the *Felicity*, in the port of Marseilles a week ago. Too early to worry, but when he does report in, we'll contact you about a rendezvous. Albert. Yes, Albert's your man, your pianist, and he'll help you set up your agent network we're calling Heckler, home-based in Lyon."

*   *   *

I had so much to commit to memory. But for now, I let go of these thoughts. My head was propped up against the train's window, the warmth of the sun rested on my neck like a warm towel, and the gentle rhythm of the tracks began to take hold. Before long, I was lost in a memory, back to the Lyon I had loved before the war: strolling the traboules, those dark arched passageways between buildings used by silk merchants centuries before. Then deeper still to that crystal day in May four years earlier. The air, so fresh and sweet; the sky, so bright and blue that I shielded my eyes by gazing down toward the low, lazy oar boats gliding without care on the Rhone. The laughter and the accordion mixing in the warm spring breeze, the open-air markets that flourished on the cobblestone streets at the river's edge, the endless fields of red poppies nodding gently in the breeze, the calls of the fish monger, the aroma of sharp cheese, the bustle of—

"*Excusez-moi. Quelqu'un est assis* à *cote de vous?*"

What *was* that noise? Something about a seat?

"*Quelqu'un est assis* à *cote de vous? Ceci est un train complet.*"

He can't be asking me. My head, pressed against the window, my eyes tight, my mind, still afloat, barely, in that liquid world. Perhaps if I ignored the words, I could climb back into my dreams.

"*Excusez-moi, Madame.*"

"*No, no, par tous les moyens, assis,*" I said, irritated. No, the seat next to me was not taken, I said, pulling my handbag closer, my head still resting on the window, my eyes now open but fixed.

A clean-shaven man was glaring at me. His moon face held small features: a pinched mouth, pressed tight, and dark eyes too narrowly spaced amidst an otherwise vacant landscape. He threw his fedora and bag onto the overhead rack with great fanfare, as if he were acting in a play. Lowering himself, he squeezed and wiggled his enormous girth onto a portion of my seat.

I forgave his encroachment but not his disagreeable aroma: cheap musk in profusion, masking—but not well enough—the wretched sourness of his body odor. I repositioned myself closer to the window and tried to be charitable—after all, it was a warm August day—but really, when he leaned over, rivulets of sweat cascaded from the corner of his right eye, and when he jockeyed for position, drops of his perspiration darkened the frontier of my blue print skirt.

He appeared to be a businessman—with a flat gold ring on the last finger of his hand and a narrow black bowtie—not the kind to frequent a second-class compartment. But like many aggressive men of his type, he seemed impervious to good manners. He continued to hound me.

"I'm Claude, Claude DuMaine," he said in French, thrusting his thick mitt close to my nose.

I turned as little as required and accepted it weakly. His hand was pink and puffy, moist like uncooked pork, and like the rest of his body, it reeked of cheap cologne.

When he lifted his paw to grasp mine, he revealed an enormous wet mark under his right arm that, at eye-level, had the salty outline of a drained swamp. "After meetings in Spain, I'm heading for France. Vichy. Contracts with the government, you know—spare parts for heavy machinery—mostly for locomotives like this one. It's easier to repair than replace one of these old engines, especially now. But you're never sure you'll get paid."

I was holding out, playing drowsy. Unsuccessfully.

"I didn't catch your name . . . Madame. Madame?"

"Virginia."

"And you are headed to France, too, Virginia, or is Barcelona your destination?"

"France," I said without enthusiasm.

"And what brings you to France?"

"To write."

"Pardon?"

"To write. I'm a writer."

"Ahhh, yes. Let me see. You are a writer of books, no? Magazines and newspapers?"

"A newspaper."

"Hmmm . . . a writer traveling through the forbidden zone. And you travel freely, back to France? You are not a citizen of France, yes? Few have the privilege to travel across the border and back, and yet your French is impeccable."

He stopped for a moment, then righted himself, sitting straight in his seat as if he were a school marm back at Roland Park. "Virginia, I'd like to play a little game with you. I pride myself on being able to guess the nationality of strangers. Now, don't tell me."

Sensing this charade would continue with or without my consent, I turned to face DuMaine.

His moon face brightened as he gave me the once-over. "You don't have the dark Latin features or the fire in your eyes like an Iberian. Nor a pale complexion like the women from Britain. No one from that country would be so unwise as to enter France these days, now would they?" DuMaine turned serious and peered into my eyes, probing for a reaction. "And yet, I am told British spies use these trains. Imagine their foolishness."

The hair on the back of my neck rose. The moment had come upon me like a sniper's bullet. I should have known. I'd trained for this, goddam it, but still hadn't seen it coming. His selection of a seat next to mine, his insistence on engaging me, his probing for personal information. All clues. My first encounter with a gestapo agent.

Unprepared and off-balance, I took and held a small, shallow breath. I'm a newswoman damn it. It's a strong story. Grab hold of it. He was so close, the man who called himself DuMaine, that he could inspect the slightest self-doubt reflected on my face. His wretched odor was disorienting.

The stakes were extraordinarily high, and it took all my powers of concentration to recover and speak as if completely unruffled. I tried to respond calmly with some warmth to embrace DuMaine lest he think I had something to hide. I looked away, only for a second, to compose myself and fill my lungs, silently, with fresh air. But my voice was dry and cracked ever so slightly. Moisture formed at my hairline.

"I . . . wouldn't know about such things, but those who are caught can't be very smart now, can they?" I added a small laugh, which bolstered my confidence. "I'm an American. And yes, I write for a newspaper in New York."

Did DuMaine sense my discomfort? Perhaps no more than the usual surprise that comes when anyone stares intently at your face, inches from his own. But did he think me a spy? I couldn't be sure. His eyes had moved on. Still, I'd feel differently, more confident, if I'd paid heed to the warning signs and had rehearsed my cover in advance. But those who live a spy's life know it takes time to invent the subtle details that, once knit together, become the unshakable story of your fabricated life.

I glanced at my watch. Several more hours before the Pyrenees. I deflected the conversation. "All these questions and yet you remain a mystery. The only clue you've offered is that you're a businessman. Now tell me, where you are from?"

"Well, Virginia, you're not playing the game, are you? You made me guess your origin. Now it's your turn. Try to guess mine."

Feeling more composed, I looked down as if in thought. "Well, let's see," I said. "Your French is not Parisian, more country French— with the barest hint of German—so you're most likely from the mountains. And you have a large, powerful physique," I added with a modest smile. "Could you be from the border between France and Germany? If pushed, I'd say you are from the Alsace."

"Yes, yes. Very well done, Virginia. A writer must be observant, and you are a good judge of people, too. It seems that we can read each other like open books. I can't help but think there are more chapters to your story," he said without emotion. "And we will open the book again at another time."

DuMaine must have collected what he needed, enough to judge the veracity of my cover, because he stopped asking questions. Our conversation turned to travel, and I began seasoning my remarks with unimportant drivel about France before the war. Then I droned on about food. Pastries. I can be boring when I choose to be. I must have succeeded in creating sufficient ennui, because DuMaine lost interest and when the conversation trailed off, I pulled *Gone with the Wind* from my handbag and propped myself up against the window.

My eyes were on the page, but my mind was on my performance. My first. Back at Beaulieu, I would have achieved a passing grade, but it occurred to me that the time for dress rehearsals was over. The curtain had risen on a netherworld where people use false names and identities and "good enough" still can get you killed. I hadn't even stepped foot in France, for God's sake. Had I aroused the gestapo's interest already?

The time of long shadows came and went. No one felt like talking, so in silence and in the dark, we passed through Barcelona and began our slow ascent up the dolomite slopes of the Pyrenees. I lowered the window to freshen the stuffy compartment, and when a crisp wind pushed my hair back, I closed it again, quickly. Peering down through the grimy glass, I noticed kerosene lamps were being lit and smoke flowed level from the few huts clinging to the mountainside. The end of summer. Soon snow would fall on the narrow mountain trails worn smooth by goats and the boots of black-marketeers. How difficult it would be then to cross these mountains. No roads, uncertain weather, little shelter, unforgiving terrain.

It was late when the train made its way down the mountains, our brakes squealing all the way until our carriage stopped abruptly. A woman in the next compartment gave a quick cry of surprise and some light packages wrapped in brown paper slid off the shelf above us. Outside, a simple white rectangular sign with green letters hung illuminated under lights with bell shades. Perpignan. We'd arrived at the entrance of the German-controlled border of France.

It was all noise and chaos on the platform, with a sea of crisp gray uniforms forming a barrier in front of the station. Though it was dark, Nazi officers seemed particularly alert: yelling orders, shoving the old or tentative, restraining hungry-looking dogs barking on short leashes.

It surprised me, that first glimpse of the enemy through the window, so many of them stretched along the length of the train. I tried not to stare but fixed momentarily on one fresh-looking face—slim, blonde, a man with delicate features—in the middle of the gray that roiled like rippling surf. Out of place and lost, the soldier couldn't have been more than seventeen, probably a new recruit, with an innocence that reminded me of John. There he stood, his uniform too large for his narrow frame. His sergeant approached and shouted in his ear. A stern look came across this young soldier as if he were screwing up his courage, and a thought, a jolting thought, rose to challenge me. Could I kill this young man?

I stayed focused, held my breath, and released it slowly, but the pulse of my heart lingered in my ears. Excitement is the twin of fear. The same heart flutter, shallow breathing, dryness of mouth. But at that moment, I wasn't certain which emotion ruled.

It couldn't have been more than a moment when I turned to Claude to say goodbye but his suitcase and hat were gone from the overhead shelf. He'd already disappeared down the steps and into the crowd.

I collected my bag from below my seat, patted the pocket in my cotton skirt—feeling for my passport and press credentials—and took one last glance at the commotion outside my window. It was dark, but just outside the beam of the platform light I caught a last glimpse of Claude. Or was I mistaken? I couldn't be certain—the man's eyes were shielded by the brim of his fedora—but it was a portly fellow speaking with a German officer by the terminal's iron gate. He nodded several times toward the train then hustled off the platform. The officer blew his whistle once, and three soldiers ran to join him. Somehow I knew they were coming for me.

Strange, at that moment I recalled Vera's raspy voice that evening in Buck's apartment: "The Germans know we're infiltrating France and can sniff out the hesitant, the partially committed, anyone who displays one speck of doubt. They're the ones we lose first."

"Identity papers, everyone must show their papers. Show them. Yes. That's right." A scuffle broke out on the platform. An old man with a battered suitcase held together with rope was beaten to the ground and hauled away. I was climbing down the stairs and paid no attention to the scene or to the German soldiers with lugers strapped to their sides, swimming through the crowd toward me.

"You!" one of them barked. "Come with us." Without waiting for a reply, they pulled me brusquely off the last stair, and hurried me toward the terminal.

Cuthbert barely kept pace. I maintained my composure, but my face felt hot and moist. Would I be searched? Why would a newswoman have so many francs strapped around her waist? My back stiffened and my bearing, more erect. It could be a difficult interrogation.

The commandant, waiting in a small windowless office, was seated behind an oak desk clear of paper. I was pushed into the seat in front of him.

"What is the meaning of this?" I demanded.

The commandant, with a lean, expressionless face and receding hairline, didn't answer. "Give me your papers," he said in a bored monotone, which seemed oddly comforting. Maybe my appearance was routine. One of many he'd see today. He glanced at my passport and press credentials, then noticing I was an American, straightened up.

"Let me see . . . Miss Virginia Hall," he said in perfect English. "Well, this is interesting. An American woman journalist coming to visit our French charges, the Vichy. Your male colleagues are right to remain in America. There isn't much to see in Vichy. Or so little that it can be handled by a woman. You aren't here to spread lies about us, are you?"

"I'm an American reporter accredited by the French government."

"Ah yes, the Vichy, but you are a guest of the German people, too." Without looking up he lifted his finger and motioned vaguely toward a door with iron bars. "And you must pass through that gate." Thumbing through my credentials, the commandant continued talking as if preoccupied. "We must preserve the peace at all costs. The French try to flee, and the agitators and spies—well, they come to upset those who remain. We can't tolerate any disruption, now can we?"

His eyes stayed low as he scanned my passport, turning my document sideways to examine the forged stamps backdated from the US. The money belt now was two notches too tight. I took a deep, silent breath. The commandant's dark eyes slid without effort from the document and fixed on my wooden companion.

Cuthbert was straight, while my right leg was bent under the chair. I hadn't changed my stump sock since Lisbon, and after the long train ride, my nub was raw and giving me fits.

The commandant had seen my ungraceful entrance. I'd stumbled into his office and now, his tired expression brightened to reflect a curious delight, as if he had discovered an odd creature at the zoo. "A lady with a fake leg. I saw you limp. A lady with a limp," he said in a tone of childish surprise. "It sounds like a song by Maurice Chevalier." Then, improbably, he broke out in a high-pitched laugh. "I can hear it now, in my head, with an accordion in the background." He continued laughing and looked at his underling who was standing at attention by the door. "Stroheim, sing a few bars for me. Lady with a limp."

Stroheim didn't respond. He looked straight ahead as the commandant continued to laugh.

"Stroheim is all work. He doesn't have my sense of humor," the commandant said with a final giggle. Then in an instant, his face tightened, and what came out was stern and forceful. "Make no mistake, Miss-Hall-with-a-limp, you are here as a guest. And we have expectations of our guests. Our guests keep away from troublemakers. Our guests sign the hotel register. We need to know where you are at all times. America has not yet made up its mind about this war, and for your sake I hope it stays that way. If that changes," he said, slowing his pace, "we will need to find you, and of course, help you make other . . . arrangements. Now, let's see what you are hiding, shall we?"

As Stroheim lifted my bag onto the desk, I heard the commandant mutter, "A fake leg. I wonder. How does it fit beneath your skirt? Where does it touch your tender skin? Let us . . ." He paused mid-thought. "No . . . But I am curious." A few more seconds passed before he declared more loudly. "I am an officer, a German officer . . . No, no, your luggage. Yes, let us find what you are smuggling into France. Stroheim, open the bag. Please."

The heat rose, but I stayed within myself. The commandant's focus had shifted from Cuthbert to my suitcase. Focus. Stay disinterested. Motionless. Had I heard him correctly? Lift my skirt for that sick Nazi bastard? The heat began to rise again. My God! I'd refuse. I began to fidget then looked at my bag. I'd fight not to be revealed that way. My eyes lifted to the corners of the ceiling. I took conscious breaths. In and out, slowly, softly. Again. Then again.

After pawing through my clothing, giving special attention to my white cotton knickers and laughing as he held them up toward the overhead lights, the Commandant pushed the jumbled mess across the desk and left me to zip it back up. Then he pointed to the door. His last words to me were bland and dull: "The gate is to the right."

I choked down my disgust and walked quickly to the exit. Cuthbert and I were safe for now, but what personal affronts or worse awaited me on the other side of that iron door? And I had another reason to fume. The commandant's interview had kept me from boarding the evening's last train to Vichy and had delayed my meetings with French and American officials, where I'd present my credentials.

As I settled in for the night on the train station's hard bench, I touched my old brooch, a smooth pink shell above my left breast.

CHAPTER TWO

_____

After the accident, Dindy told me her father, who had died years
before, came to her in a vision. They were in a rocking chair. He
took her in his arms and said she could join him if it was too awful
but that her mother still needed her. She got better after that. Was
Dindy a religious person? No.

LORNA CATLING
VIRGINIA HALL'S NIECE

DECEMBER 1933, SMYRNA, TURKEY

My ambition never was to be a spy. In the early 1930s I was a clerk in the US State Department with thoughts of becoming an ambassador. My friends said it was a silly, impossible dream, because in those days there were no women ambassadors, and only six of several thousand diplomats were women. I thought it stupid and absurd there were so few of us. For Christ's sake, women had been voting for over a decade and it was high time a window was opened into that stuffy club. I had stronger credentials than most—spoke three languages, travelled extensively overseas, graduated from Consular Academy in Vienna. The Foreign Service seemed the right step forward. I was headstrong and determined, and to prepare for the Foreign Service test, I studied late into the night. Oh, I suppose I was caught up in the adventure of being overseas, being in charge, in the thick of it. I was young, stubborn, and absolutely convinced I'd make it into the diplomatic corps and rise to the rank of ambassador no matter how long it took.

My first post was Warsaw, but Smyrna, Turkey is the assignment I remember most.

*   *   *

Old Smyrna was on a peninsula of rolling land, lakes, and mountains surrounded by an expansive sea—a land shrouded in myth, the home of Alexander the Great, the birthplace of Homer. As a consulate clerk, I had time to pursue the outdoor life that I loved.

December 8, 1933, began as a day like any other. Four embassy friends and I left work early for an afternoon hunt.

Maria and Tod; Tod's wife, Elaine; my beau Emil, a young army officer at the Polish embassy, and I met in the Gediz delta just north of Izmir. It was there, in the low-lying tidal flats, that the gallinago—a plump bird, with a long curved beak—hunted for worms and small crustaceans. We arrived when the sun, past its zenith, had begun to call the birds to settle in the reeds along the edge of the estuary.

We talked, as most young State Department people do, about events of the day, and our conversation turned to Germany and the rise of a most unlikely new chancellor, a failed artist-turned-politician whose hate-filled speeches were becoming popular. Tod, a sturdy lad with a fresh-scrubbed face and sandy hair, said his friends at the British embassy didn't think the chancellor a threat. War wasn't very likely. If it did come, well then, Germany would fight Russia. Maria agreed, and each of us quickly followed suit. We spoke with youthful certainty that any war would be safely contained. And the United States? We'd stay far, far away.

All of us nodded in blissful unity—all, that is, except Emil. He was quiet for a while. I suppose everyone was waiting for him to agree with the rest of us, but in waiting, he was thinking how best to tell us we were wrong. And when Emil spoke, his words came out like steam escaping from a teakettle. He called us naïve. The persecution of the Jews, he said, was fueling the rise of a new world order filled with bigotry and intolerance. Worse still, he predicted the chancellor would push the boundaries of his country. It would lead to a war that would enflame all of Europe and the US, too. We laughed, poked fun at him, called him excitable Emil full of gloom and doom. But I now see our cavalier certainty was based on nothing but false hope. Perhaps we wanted to wish away the cruelty toward the Jews and the growing power of this new chancellor, as if by ignoring the warning signs the world would take care of itself. But Emil had seen German aggression before, and his eyes were aflame as he spoke. He knew. Emil knew of the gathering storm.

*   *   *

Emil. I'd almost forgotten. How long ago that was—our lives together before my life was cleaved in two.

Emil, his firm jaw, taut olive skin and hair like midnight, his slight British accent, his majestic bearing and strong arms and hands. He worked with wood, a carpenter whose body was shaped and hardened by the tools of his trade. A woodworker-turned-diplomat. He loved the natural world as I did. We were inseparable. A pair of bookends.

That week in Izmir, we borrowed an old jalopy, drove through the rugged hills outside Smyrna, and spoke of the animals and plants. As I held onto my wide-brimmed hat tightly against the warm breeze rising up the face of the mountain, Emil pointed to a harrier high above, calling it Kirkos, an ancient name meaning circular flight. In the back seat, a wicker basket with cloth napkins overflowed with different fruit and cheeses.

After hiking the highlands, it was time for lunch. His head in my lap, we fed each other tart grapes. The ancient laurels with their gnarled trunks and glossy leaves shielded us from the midday sun, and in their cool shade we drank glasses of red wine as we looked over the city of Smyrna by the sea.

"Tell me about your home in Maryland," Emil said. "Does it have the sun of Turkey? The hills overlooking the Aegean? The food, fit for the gods of Homer? Most of all, does it have someone there like me?"

"Well," I said, "it has the sun that shines over the Chesapeake— the most splendid waterway on the East coast with all the fresh fish and game birds you could ever want. It has the Catoctin Mountains, which might not be as lofty as the hills around Smyrna, but they're covered in a light green blanket in the spring, and in the fall, they turn orange and gold like the setting sun. But does Maryland have someone like you? I'm sure there might be—in my future."

Emil grabbed me, and we wrestled to the blanket, where he pinned me down until I confessed that Maryland didn't have anyone like him.

Later in the evening when the tide was low and far from shore, we walked the beach. Emil carried an old canvas backpack with leather straps filled with more fruit and wine. Our sunset dinner. He collected driftwood as I sat on the sand, my arms wrapped around my knees, my face toward the reddened sky, the slightly damp sand clinging to my feet, and the sound of waves breaking before us. He returned with an armful of wood, and I opened a bottle of wine. Emil, sorting through the pieces, showed me the more unusual ones.

The wine loosened our tongues and freed our imaginations. "This stick looks like a fish—see?" said Emil. "This knot is the eye, and the grain of the wood the scales?" Then he offered another that had a human-looking face and said, "Tell me, who does this look like?" He knew what I would say.

"Why, that's my boss, old Ambassador Skinner, of course!" I said. "Or you in a few years."

Emil frowned and acted hurt. "I thought you had just one ounce of affection for me," he said.

After stacking the wood to a height of his thigh, he pulled out his lighter and set flame to some dried cattails he tucked beneath. The yellow and orange tongues licked the wood, and the branches cracked and popped. Red sparks littered the sky like a thousand burning diamonds. And as the last point of the sun slid beneath the horizon, the fire grew brighter—yet not so bright as to dim the heavens.

Alone in the dark with only the fire and stars to illuminate us, we were transported a thousand years earlier, and we imagined that by some natural calamity, we were the only two people left in the world. No one else, no job to go back to, just us, and we were only responsible for ourselves. Not a frightening thought but a comforting one. It was enough that we were together. Just us. The world could just curl up and blow away for all we cared.

As we drank a second bottle of red, the fire's coals were burning down, the low flame, hot and blue. I was about to finish my glass when Emil pulled me closer, looked me in the eye, and placed his mouth tenderly on mine. His face then his neck so close, his scent so masculine, like my herb garden back home, of sandalwood and clove.

As we reclined in the sand, I told him what I liked, but he told me to hush. He knew.

Emil began slowly and with caring, to massage those secret places and told me how he loved my body, long and lean. His strong arm, fully extended, touched my calves then slowly with the back of his hand teased them lightly, moving upward until he reached my thighs, working the right then the left. His hands, so unyielding, drifted over my hills and valleys, using just the right pressure, then with increasing urgency. The fever spread and our pace quickened.

I rose to my knees and tugged at his belt, tore through his garments, then made him groan and arch his back. Then he pulled away, lowered me to the ground and broke through my remaining clothing, favoring me, deliciously, as I had him.

Near the summit, the sandalwood and clove now filled me completely, his firm hands all about, my forehead hot and moist. I mounted Emil greedily, gripping his hips with the flesh of my thighs. Then I plunged my carriage forward again and again, and there we stayed, on the crest of the wave, until Emil's eyes squeezed tightly and his mouth opened, and I quickened the pace so the wave's power would overtake us both. In the fury, our bodies stiffened. We cried out with mild obscenities in unison, then separately. But then as quickly as it came, the wave receded, and I collapsed onto Emil's panting chest. There I stayed until I regained enough strength to roll off.

Once on my back, fully spent, the fingers on my right hand, the only extremity not paralyzed by pleasure, reached the sand, working it mindlessly. My first finger and thumb hit the edge of a small object, worn almost flat and smooth, a shell. Its small pink interior glinted in the fire like a tiny star. I gazed at it then held it tightly, a memento. Proof that in that moment, I lived in a time and place where love and completeness were possible, and if only for an instant, I could be transformed into something larger, something eternal.

Emil asked to see my prize. I said yes and handed it to him gladly. He surprised me one week later, returning the translucent pink shell, small and misshapen as it was, with a small gold clasp.

He'd returned it fashioned as a brooch.

*   *   *

The muddy estuary of Izmir on the Aegean reminded me of the eastern shore of the Chesapeake where I had hunted mallards many times before. On my eighteenth birthday, my father Ned gave me one of his prize possessions—a twelve-gauge Browning side-load with a carved walnut stock—now loaded and ready at my side.

The frenzied screech of the gallinago was growing louder, as the five of us approached the shore where silty water had divided and spilled into rivulets, then drained with slow precision into the huge expanse of the delta. Closer to shore amid the mud, where we were to hunt, the reeds and tall, feathered grasses grew.

Our talk turned serious. "You know, Emil, the State Department doesn't have many women diplomats. You could almost count them on one hand. And none are ambassadors."

"Perhaps," he said, "but you'll show them. You have the heart of a lion. They cannot deny you. You'll see."

To our left, the December sun slipped lower in the sky. Little more than an hour of light remained. The north wind began to pick up and blow against my cheek, turning it rosy, but I had my long, gray tweed jacket with a patch of leather at my right shoulder to keep me warm.

Emil laughed at my hunting gloves. I'd cut off the fingers so I could feel wood stock around the barrel and the steel trigger. It was my connection, organic and real, with my prey. And while I had sympathy for the gallinago, the bird exposed itself—made itself vulnerable. That was its fault, its nature, and taking advantage in the hunt was mine.

The five of us headed together in a line walking slowly, separated, twenty-five feet apart. The tide was beginning to withdraw, and all that remained was the thick, sticky mud with just enough water to make the sucking sound of our boots releasing slowly from that viscous earth. It was difficult to stand. The few gallinago we encountered flushed horizontal to the line, left and into the setting sun. They were too quick, which surprised us, and none got off a good shot. We were too preoccupied with our footing.

"The gallinago flush like quail," Emil said, "quick and erratic."

I had hunted quail and expected a difficult shot but not the unsteady footing. The reeds in the tidal estuary hid us from one another and Emil and I were alone except for the sounds of the marsh: the wind rustling through the grass, the screech of the nesting shorebirds, and the suction of our boots freeing from the mud.

There was movement in the tall grass. Someone shouted "Damn!" followed by a quick laugh. Maria had lost her balance and Tod and Emil went to lift her from the earthy muck.

"Not much good today, am I?" she asked.

Ahead lay a single strand of barbed wire between two posts fashioned from weathered branches. Maria, righted, seemed in good humor. As if to prove her spirit intact, she moved forward briskly and was the first to navigate the wire. Handing her gun to Tod, she climbed over, nearly catching her foot, then motioned to me.

I pushed the wire down with my right hand, my shotgun under my left arm. As I lifted my left leg, my hand slipped, and the strand caught the toe of my boot. Off-balance, I hopped once, then stumbled. The trigger to my twelve-gauge caught the folds of my coat, and the gun discharged.

I don't remember much more. It was like an old movie in one of my father's theaters. Time slowed, and I became an observer from above. My disbelief arrived just an instant before the searing pain. I do recall seeing the bone above my left ankle splinter like a tree in a mighty storm and a stain, like a crimson ink blot, expanded at the base of my tweed coat. The soft, cold mud began to ooze around my face and enter the corner of my mouth. I tried to close it, but my lips wouldn't move.

Maria later told me there was little time to spare, and Tod said

Emil directed the others much as a military officer might in the heat of battle. Soon after the gun discharged, they said my lips turned blue, and I was growing cold to the touch. Elaine called to me, but I couldn't speak. It was serious, she said, mostly because of my eyes. They looked lost, aimless, and began to roll. I'm told Emil took the red cotton scarf from his neck and wrapped it around my leg just under my knee. Then he found a sturdy stick under the reeds and tied the ends of the scarf around it, twisting the stick hard. Again and again to cut the flow. Still, blood was streaming from my wound and pooling in the mud. Brown and red. Everywhere brown and red.

No one panicked. Emil took off his coat to use as a stretcher, and together, very slowly, they lifted me from the mud. Tod said he became worried only after Maria's face seemed to drain of blood almost as quickly as mine. But she kept the stick tight, though it took forever to pull me from the muck.

Just before my vision blurred and I blacked out, a calm came over me. That's the way it is when you bleed out. It is the easiest way to die. I'd see it later, many times—too many times—in France. No anxiety, no hysteria. After the surprise comes the cold, then shivers, then stillness. Though I couldn't call out, my mind seemed quiet and clear. Strange, I was thinking of Box Horn Farm. Father, who had passed years before, was rocking on the front porch. I was in his arms, and when he spoke, he called me by my childhood name.

"Now Dindy," he said, "you've got to stay awake a little while longer. Your mother needs you. If you must, you can come home with me, but only after you try the very best you can."

CHAPTER THREE

Too many of my friends were killed because they talked too much.
Virginia Hall

AUGUST 1941, VICHY, FRANCE

On the early morning train from Perpignan to Vichy, I stared for hours, fixed and unfocused, on the silhouettes that drifted by. My head, pressed against the dusty window, bobbed and swayed to the demands of the rail, and though desperate for sleep, I couldn't find it. The fire within had subsided, but the commandant's childish laugh echoed in my mind, and the memory clung to my skin like a filthy fog I wanted desperately to wash away.

I couldn't stand to admit it, but for all the disgust brought by the encounter, the commandant spoke a single truth: America had not made its mind up about the war.

The proof was there for all to see. The news clips at the cinema in Southampton: the crowds at New York's Madison Square Garden. Thousands standing, cheering Charles Lindbergh—hero of cross-Atlantic flight, friend of Hitler, and admirer of the German Luftwaffe. Even the headline of *Le Monde*, opened on the seat beside me, confirmed it: "Americans Demand Roosevelt Stay Out of Europe's War." How alone the Brits were in this desperate hour. So little hope. No cavalry coming to the rescue.

I reached my destination, the Hotel Thermala on Rue Jardet, by midmorning. Like all buildings in Vichy, this once grand concrete structure was soot covered and now falling apart. I walked the threadbare runner up a marble staircase to the reception area, where worn velvet drapes blocked the sun from entering two-story arched windows. Overhead, cobwebs collected between the crystals of the chandelier, which remained unlit. But no one seemed to notice or care. Disrepair had become the norm.

I was desperate to bathe and tend to Cuthbert. My wooden companion had been strapped to me ever since Lisbon and was needier than a colicky infant. I couldn't blame him; no privacy on that crowded train, then a fitful night dozing in the station. There was no way to soothe him or tend to his needs.

But Cuthbert was predictable in his irritation, demanding my attention by focusing his anger on my hips, where his harness, cinched tight, bruises them. Cuthbert refused to yield and ground into my stump with each step. He made me pay for ignoring him by turning it raw and painfully swollen, as if shards of glass were slicing deeply into my most sensitive skin.

He wouldn't let me forget, either, our early days, when we first met at Box Horn Farm and I tried to make him bend to my will. The infection he caused damn near killed me. But that was early in our relationship, and since then we'd established a truce: I'd try to be more respectful, and he wouldn't be so hurtful. Now we understood each other enough to know we needed our own space. Time away. Time to regroup.

When the time came to lean Cuthbert against the wall, I lingered in the bath. It was self-indulgent, but who could fault me? The feeling of liberation was glorious, being immersed in warm liquid after being on that damn train. The sweat and grime dissolved from my skin leaving it moist and fresh, and after patting my nub dry, I gently massaged it with Noxzema. Outside my window, the leaves on the plane trees were swaying gently and the sun was not yet high or hot. I chose a blue-checked muslin dress for my meeting to present my press credentials at Vichy's Town Hall a few blocks away.

It was a short walk down Rue Jardet to the large structure with a simple face. The matronly woman at the front desk took my name, then pointed behind her, to a cavernous waiting area, which appeared larger than it was, because I was the only one there. After fifteen minutes, I began tapping my right foot, and an hour after that Madame entered and said I should follow her to a back room.

I was about to give someone a piece of my mind when I was met by a bureaucrat behind a polished oak counter, whose clothes hung about him as if still on a hanger—a ghost of a man not wholly in the moment or of this world, and my anger at once seemed trivial. His head drooped toward the ground like a wilted tulip, and his round shoulders bent forward as if pulled down by some enormous weight. His eyes, dull and vacant, his face, sallow and without expression, told me a tremendous sadness had entered his life. How difficult and wearying it must be, trapped and deprived of hope in your own homeland.

He took my papers silently, and without looking up, embossed my press card with a raised seal and returned it. On departing, I tried to meet his eyes with my own, but his head stayed low, and neither of us said a word. I stashed my credentials in my purse and hurried out the door.

My British colleagues had told me to avoid Americans and by no means reveal my mission to the embassy staff. The smaller the circle, they said, the more likely I'd remain undetected by Vichy or German authorities. Still, as a US citizen, I was required to register, and doing so supported my cover as a journalist. If America entered the war, the embassy would tell us to leave at once. I'd ignore their advice, of course, and remain in France to continue my clandestine work.

I entered the embassy's ornately carved wooden doors and was greeted by the charge d' affaires, who said Ambassador William Leahy had been called away unexpectedly and wouldn't return for some time. Instead, I should see the vice consul in Lyon, a short train ride away.

This didn't bother me in the least. Lyon was my ultimate destination, so I packed my belongings and departed the hotel.

I took the 1:45, and on arrival, I was ushered to the third-floor corner suite of the vice consul. George Wittinghill's office, paneled in French oak, was decorated with Louis XV furniture. A fine blue and white porcelain vase with fresh cut red roses rested on a highly polished circular table in the room's center, and off to the right in the corner, a telescope pointed out the floor-to-ceiling arched window to the street below. A free-standing globe looked out of place in a distant corner, and soft music—Debussy I thought—drifted from a horn phonograph atop a garish corner stand.

My eyes shifted to Wittinghill, a tall reed of a man in a charcoal morning coat and red Jacquard tie, seated behind a large mahogany desk. His head was bowed toward his *Pariser Zeitung* even after I entered. No welcome. No introduction.

He got to the point, though his eyes stayed fixed on his paper. "Blast it all. Just what I need. A reporter. My dear girl, you're not going to make things difficult for me, are you?"

Momentarily disoriented, my reaction, a reflex really, was to offer an equally flippant response. No more difficult than the life of the average Frenchman, I'd say. It was on my lips, but I held it and began to observe.

Wittinghill. What a twit. I'd never know why they placed such pompous men in posts of some consequence. Especially there in Lyon with Vichy officials and German officers. Then my mind turned ever so slightly. Vichy officials and Germans. Who did he know? Maybe Wittinghill did have something to offer after all. I'd explore him a bit. Probe the boundary of his knowledge and perhaps secure an introduction.

But how should I proceed? I'd go slow. Ease his concerns. Massage his pride. Soothe his vanity. He could be full of bluster and have nothing for me. Then I'd depart quickly like a fine mist without feeding his anger or provoking any emotion. Nothing tangible for him to remember. Nothing to hang onto. Not even a memory.

"I'm sorry, I don't understand what you mean."

"Oh, I think you do," Wittinghill said. "But let me spell it out for you anyway." His eyes hovered above the edge of the newspaper. "These past months have been extraordinarily difficult for us here in Lyon. After Paris stumbled, moving the embassy to Vichy and assuming new responsibilities at this consulate has been an excruciating experience that has tried the patience of our entire staff. We've made the best of it by working hard to develop a strong relationship with the Vichy government, Marshall Petain and Pierre Laval and their personal representative, the governor-general. We have exceptionally good relations with our German associates here in Lyon, too. Exceptionally good. My colleagues and I have, well, we've developed a—" Wittinghill groped momentarily, then let the words slip casually from his lips—"a relationship of mutual trust. And yes, on occasion, that trust goes beyond our diplomatic instruction." His words were crisp and officious. "The last thing I want is to jeopardize my personal associations by having to make excuses for why some American *journalist* is poking her nose into places where it doesn't belong. Am I making myself clear?"

No, I wasn't listening to his blather. I was still considering Wittinghill's potential as an unwitting source. As the vice consul continued to prattle on, I tried to retrieve a memory, a briefing in Beaulieu about officials I was likely to meet in Lyon. Wittinghill. What was it about Wittinghill? I remembered the Brits were suspicious of Wittinghill and especially his associate, *Houston*? Yes. Suspicious of both Wittinghill and Houston. Houston, they had said, harbored pro-German views. "If they know your mission," the briefer warned, "they could work against you."

"I understand it must have been challenging for you," I said, warming up to the vice consul. "Moving from Paris to Vichy and Lyon. The life of a consular official, experiencing all that stress. Working to bring hope to the French people while the Germans are looking over your shoulder."

"Well, Miss Hall," Wittinghill said, standing up. He folded his paper and put it down on the desk, then hesitated and his demeanor softened. "Of course, it's been very difficult for all of us here."

"That's precisely the kind of story . . ." I paused as if in thought, then murmured just loudly enough, ". . . that might be . . ." I raised my voice. "Yes. The right angle for my readers in New York. A day in the life of a senior embassy official. The *New York Evening Post* has a broad circulation. Over a million. There could be a story in there."

"I'm not blind to what's going on, but you, your readers, have to understand. This is a very delicate situation. I'm working my contacts to ease conditions for the French people, but that will take a while. Time, Miss Hall, time. The world of diplomacy is built on time and patience," he said, thrusting his chin in the air. "That *is* something your readers need to know. In the meantime, it's our policy, the policy of our country, to remain neutral. That means we treat both sides with courtesy and respect."

"We'll need to take pictures, of course."

"Well, I don't know," Wittinghill said, stroking his chin.

"One or two, in your office, you behind the desk. I can't commit the paper, but I think a feature could work. We'd focus on the French side, how you're using diplomacy to help the French people. A humanitarian angle. But for this story to have a chance of flying with my editors, to give it life, I'll need to speak to some of your colleagues in the Vichy government—with your permission and support, of course."

"Well, I'm not sure," he said straightening his tie. "I could check with the counsel general. We'd need to bring him onboard." Wittinghill looked down for a moment then raised his eyes, which had brightened. "Yes. I can see where such an article might have some merit."

The hook set, I changed the subject, allowing him to spray like a geyser on his love of the French classics: Berlioz, Ravel, and Faure. I let the line run out a bit longer and then made my way to the door.

"Very good then," I said. "I know you are a busy man, and I need to be off, but let me give you a call in a few days. That should give you enough time to contact your Vichy associates. Three of your most senior contacts should do, and then I'll follow up with interviews. Oh, yes, one more thing. I was hoping to set up a letterbox at the consulate. I'll be moving around and need a regular postal address. Can that be arranged?"

"I don't see why not. I'll have Miss Darby set it up for you."

I reached out my hand. "Goodbye, Mr. Wittinghill. I enjoyed meeting you."

He grasped it tightly and shook it with vigor.

As I headed out the door, the vice consul called to me. "How may I reach you presently? Where will you be staying?"

"I've just arrived, and my accommodations are unsettled. Let me contact you."

"You will have an exceedingly difficult time finding a room in Lyon, I assure you," he said, shaking his head disapprovingly. "So many refugees from the occupied zone flooding in. The Germans tell me they will reduce the flow, but God only knows how they plan to do it."

I turned my back and waved. I wasn't concerned about accommodations. Before I departed London, Jacques de Guelis, head of SOE reconnaissance, had given me the names of several contacts he'd gathered from an injured RAF pilot shot down over Lyon the previous spring. After the sun set, I'd make my first call.

Departing the embassy, I was startled by a shrill police whistle. It seems a round-up was underway—something I had heard about but had never witnessed. The Vichy police were moving in from all sides of the street, capturing Frenchmen like minnows in a net, using clubs on those who resisted, then loading them onto waiting wagons.

Vera had told me that despite their armistice with France, the Germans continued taking prisoners of war for their munitions factories and labor camps. More than a million were toiling away there already, and with the agreement of the Petain government, thousands more were being rounded up and shipped like cattle to Germany. No opportunity to return home to pick up clothes or even a toothbrush, no chance to say goodbye to wives or lovers.

I hadn't witnessed a public beating, and yet there it was, being dispensed in such a casual and routine way, as if the police were thrashing wheat. Vera had told me that the men lucky enough to escape round-ups fled to the hills of the surrounding countryside where they gathered, protected and fed by the locals.

"Their numbers now are small but growing," Vera said, "and when the time's right, they'll be a good source of recruits for intelligence collection and sabotage operations. The people call them scrub-brush. The word the French use is 'maquis.'"

I moved away from the shouts of that chaotic scene and walked toward the Rhone with purpose, as if late for an appointment. The gestapo was less likely to stop and search me if it looked like I had a destination. But really, I was waiting for the cover of night. Then I'd make my way to the Missionary Sisters of St. Mary.

Major de Guelis had told me of a priest who could help. Abbe Alesh was known to British military intelligence, MI-6, as a courier who spirited clandestine messages between the loosely knit members of French opposition groups. He lived in a convent near the confluence of the Rhone and Saone rivers and would allow me to stay for a day or two, to get my bearings before seeking more permanent accommodations.

Darkness was beginning to fall on Lyon, and though it was a warm summer night, few were strolling the cobblestone Quai Jean-Jacques Rousseau that bordered the Saone. How strange. Lyon was filled with refugees, but the town at dusk was mostly shuttered. Gone were the music and laughter of my memory, the great cacophony of life cascading onto the street, the clatter of glasses, the smoky aroma of burning Gauloise mixed with spilled wine. The Germans were in the cafes now, heads erect in their starched uniforms, leaning back, observing those who dared to venture out.

When the sun had set, I began my approach to the convent. I had no proof I was being watched, but with the memory of DuMaine still fresh, I wasn't going to take a chance. I walked through cafes, retraced my steps, back-tracked along my route, and used the reflection of shop windows in the dimming light to see if others were observing me. After a couple of hours of this purposeful wandering, practicing my countersurveillance skills and certain I was free of tails, I made my way up the convent's stone steps, worn smooth by the faithful. For this contact, Major de Guelis had instructed me to use the Marcel formula.

I held my breath and knocked on the imposing dark oak door with large black hinges and waited. It seemed I hadn't hit it hard enough. I looked around and knocked again. No response. The third time, I banged hard on the door, loudly enough for any passerby to hear.

A small portal in the middle door opened. I spoke first. "Is the abbe in?"

"Who?"

"The abbe," I said, raising my voice. "Is he in?" I looked to the street.

"Yes, I am he."

"May I look at your newspaper? I seem to have left mine with Marcel on the bus."

There was a pregnant pause.

"My newspaper is with Marcel on the bus," I said more loudly, looking around.

A round forehead tilted upward and two eyes peered at me just above the lower rim of the door's square opening. The quizzical eyes straightened. "Ahhh, why yes. Yes, you may. Marcel just returned with a new one from Nice." The abbe opened the door just wide enough for me to enter.

Abbe Alesh was short and broad in a brown robe with a rope belt around his waist. His face was round and jolly, but the corners of his eyes drooped, making him look strangely sad. "Come in, come in, quickly, quickly," he said. He stuck his head out the door, briefly looking up and down the street before pushing the latch shut. "You can't be too careful. The gestapo has agents all around. And the secret police—our own people beholden to their Nazi masters. They are especially active at night. You must be very careful. Lyon is a dangerous place."

His voice then lifted as if he were relieved. "Well, welcome. It is Germaine, yes? I've been waiting for you. Our friends didn't tell me precisely when you would arrive. I was expecting you yesterday."

"I was delayed."

The abbe brought me into a room with a gray stone floor and a semi-circular fireplace black with soot. Liquid in an iron pot was simmering above a small circle of smoldering coals. Stools surrounded a rough-hewn oak table in the center of the dimly lit room. He opened the cupboard and pulled out a sausage covered in flour, then poured me a glass of vin rouge from a nearly empty bottle on the table.

"Sit . . . sit," Alesh said. "You must be hungry from your travels. I'd offer you more but . . ." His voice trailed away. "Now tell me where you are from. Your accent, you must be from Canada. That is what I think. All I know is your name, 'Germaine,' which isn't your real name now, is it?"

I said nothing. The abbe appeared nervous and excited. I let him talk.

"You know the gestapo has been active in Lyon, looking for men who are loitering. For the work camps. But those arriving with luggage, they are the first to come under suspicion. Especially carrying two suitcases—clothes in one and the other, a wireless. More agents are coming, and the gestapo knows it. Be careful, Germaine. People meeting in cafes are being watched. You never know who is your friend. And the secret police, those bastards— may God forgive me—they are worse than the gestapo. They're everywhere. They know the people who live here. Who looks different. They can pick out the foreign face. I can help you. But only so far. If you are turned over to the gestapo—well then, only God can help you."

I nodded.

"I must tell you. There was a man sitting where you are right now. Here, two weeks ago. Albert is the name I was told to call him. He had just arrived from Gibraltar by sea to the Cotes d' Azur and made his way north. But. . ." the abbe sighed, "he said the gestapo already was looking for him. Picked him up in Marseilles for questioning. Albert said his false credentials got him past border guards, but his cover story as a businessman from Belgium was too thin. And of course, every man here is suspect."

I didn't care that British military intelligence, the MI-6, trusted the abbe. Being new, I didn't trust anyone. I acted indifferent to his news, heeded Vera's advice and spoke very little. But as the abbe continued talking, I thought more about Buck's words. The chase for Albert was on. My pianist had been tripped up, flushed from the bushes, and was being hunted by the gestapo. Already, he'd become a lesson. A cautionary tale. I ate my sausage. Sipped my wine.

"It is bad luck to be under suspicion," said the abbe. "I gave him food and stored his suitcase, but I could not allow him to stay overnight. Once the gestapo takes notice, well, even a priest cannot be seen with such a man."

The abbe's head began to sink as he revealed more of Albert's story. How Albert had shown up at his door late at night, afraid, shaking, a lost sheep among the wolves. How the abbe, a man of God, failed to bring Albert back to the fold. And now my pianist was alone, abandoned, exposed. Vulnerable.

The abbe's voice cracked. "A man becomes desperate when he knows he is the hunted. The eyes become hollow and empty. Albert was shaking like an animal hiding in the bushes waiting for the beast to pass."

Alesh put his elbows on the table, his body sagged forward, and his head slumped between his hands. Then he looked up, his eyes filled, and his voice grew low, as if he was about to confess a mortal sin. "Albert asked to be shown the chapel. He knelt before the cross. His hands clenched tight. White. Begging for deliverance. But the gestapo is the beast, and the beast never loses the scent of the kill." Words seemed caught in the abbe's throat. Then he blurted, "I am not like the Christ. I am a lowly priest. A fallen man." A drop fell on the table. "I denied Albert. I cast him out."

It took several moments for Abbe Alesh to regain his composure. I stayed silent, refusing to offer words of comfort or reveal my interest in Albert.

Wiping his eyes with the flesh of his hand, Alesh said, "You, Germaine, you are clean, and you are a woman in a convent. You may stay several nights, but then you must leave." He sniffled once. "I have two rules: don't attract the attention of the authorities, and the convent door closes at six-thirty p.m."

I nodded, but my mind was on Albert. Discovered, burned, or worse. The abbe had nothing to be ashamed of. He'd acted properly, not in his Catholic world, but in my business, we're taught to walk away when the risks became too great. I had some sympathy for the abbe, living in the middle of this turmoil, offering his services to people he didn't know and who could betray him to the gestapo. A difficult life. Who can you trust? Albert had revealed himself to the abbe. But I wouldn't.

I shifted in my seat and acted disinterested. "And where is this Albert now?"

"I do not know. Still on the run, perhaps with the secret police or, may God help him, the gestapo."

I didn't ask again. After finishing another slice of the sausage and the last sip of wine, I asked to be shown to my room.

"I see you are a lady with a limp. May I help you with your bag?"

"I carry my own bags."

"Germaine, you must remember, the phone lines are tapped, telegrams and letters are opened, and everyone is under suspicion." Alesh then said in a somber tone, "I help carry papers for others, the French who wish to remain hidden. Between the French resistance network Gloria and the Frenchman they call Lucas. I am here in this Abbey in Lyon, but I'm also a part-time Vicar in St. Hilarie parish in Paris. So you see, I have reason to travel from Lyon across the line to the occupied zone. The Germans may search others, but remove the garments of a man of God? No. This has not happened. I have much to offer. A lowly priest from Lyon can help a spy from England."

Cuthbert had been biting my stump all day. I snapped at the abbe. "Never mention that country across the Channel, even in conversations you believe are beyond the ears of the gestapo. It's 'chez nous' when we wish to speak of it." My voice turned low. "I may call on you." The words rolled quietly off my lips in a sad, almost regretful way. I was thinking of Albert. On the run, possibly in prison, or worse. The abbe was right. It would be dangerous to be associated with Albert, but I had to find him, collect his wireless, and arrange an escape from France.

"I'll start looking for new accommodations in the morning," I said.

Ruminating on Albert's fate, finding and rescuing him seemed a monumental task. I was so new to this world of espionage. I couldn't walk away from my partner but where to begin? De Guelis had given me the names of three people in a city of 400,000 filled with secret police and gestapo agents. Just three people who could be trusted. There was a sourness churning in my stomach. I was alone and floating on a raft in a hostile sea. No way to call home. No one coming to rescue me if I fell into trouble like Albert.

The abbe led me to a tiny room in a square tower at one end of the convent of cloistered nuns on the verdant hillside rising from the Saone just above where it met the Rhone. The room was spare—a single bed with a tarnished gold crucifix over a dark oak headboard and a wash basin—but I had a magnificent view of the city, and the undivided attention of a strong north wind. After a day of walking the cobblestone streets, it was a relief to remove my wooden companion.

I unharnessed Cuthbert and leaned him against the nightstand; the leather straps, lightened and hardened by sweat and salt, dangled from his side. In candlelight, Cuthbert looked like a large toy soldier—an iron major, straight, tough, and unyielding. Now beside me on that hard, penitential bed, he was at parade rest, and I was tending to my stump with mentholated cream. I never minded the medicinal aroma that came from its oils, and that night, I breathed in deeply and held the cleansing vapors. And when my lungs were about to burst, I pushed out the collected anger and evil of the past few days.

I looked up at my reflection in the mirror standing in the corner of the room. Bent forward, working my stump.

It had been years since my accident in the marshes of the Gediz; still sometimes when I saw my nub from a different angle—the scar across its face—my thoughts would drift, and I would wonder: Is that really me? Where's the rest of my leg?

I would tell myself I'm past the anger. But the disappointment would linger. I should be over it by now, I would say, and a wave of sadness would wash over me. Sometimes, if I was tired and alone and my resistance was low, my eyes would moisten. I hated myself for it, the self-pity, but then I would go deeper, trying to make sense of it all. Where would I be—no, *who would I be* if Gediz had never happened? On the ladder to ambassador? Traveling the world? Or perhaps with Emil?

CHAPTER FOUR

Miss Hall could become a fine career girl in the Consular Service.

CORDELL HULL
US SECRETARY OF STATE

JANUARY 1934, ISTANBUL

The doctor in his white lab coat said I had been drifting in and out of consciousness for days. "When your friends brought you in, you were in rough shape," he said. "They saved your life."

I can still smell that musty marsh. Dried mud was everywhere—with bits of that straw grass caked on my face, in my ears and mouth. And my wound—what a mess.

When I woke up, I wasn't shocked as much as surprised. The shock came later. At first, I looked down at the blanket covering my legs. My right leg was like the ridge of the Appalachian Mountains, proud and strong but the left, below the knee? The blanket was just as flat as the Chesapeake on a hot and airless day.

I searched the bedsheet with both hands and cried out, "My God, there's nothing there!" Then came the wild shouts. "My leg! Where is it? What have you done with my leg?" But it was gone. Gangrene. Gangrene grabbed hold of my limb and took it away. In the emptiness of the moment, I began sobbing uncontrollably, my hands covering my eyes and the tracks of wetness cascading down my face.

"There, there, Miss Hall," the doctor said, putting his hand on my shoulder. "It was a good trade—yes, a very good trade—your leg for your life."

For the longest time, I thought it would have been best if my friends had left me to bleed out in that godforsaken marsh. What the doctor had said—that nothing could be done to save my leg—I hoped to God that was true. My doctor had lots of practice with his saw in the Great War. But did I believe him? No. No I didn't. Doctors who served in that dreadful struggle were more expert in severing limbs than saving them.

It was an emotional time, the weeping and the anger, and I seemed powerless to control any of it. I suppose it was for the best that I was inaccessible, resident for the next two months in the American hospital in Istanbul—a large institution painted white to hide its appalling state of decay. Each of the thirty beds on the top-floor ward was separated by a gauzy cotton screen that established the fiction of privacy. I overheard the most intimate medical conversations, and I'm sure others heard mine.

My public surroundings did little to cheer my mood, as I was desperate to put the pieces of my life together. I hated being tightly packed with all those sick and bandaged people. Hated everything about it. All I wanted was to reclaim my life and get on with it, but that was impossible. I needed time to heal, and the hospital in Istanbul, as much as I protested, was the place to start. But it was all so exhausting—the relentless questions that intruded from deep inside. What life could I have, a woman with one leg? Would people disregard me? And during my darkest moments came the hardest question of all: Could I be loved?

My future seemed so abstract, so bleak and uncertain, especially at night, alone. Those were the most difficult times, sorting through it all imagining what the loss of my limb really meant and how my life would change, forever.

The unseasonably warm Saturday afternoon of Emil's visit, the heat was rising and forming clouds in the west. The humidity was so great that I knew, instinctively, the rain soon would fall. Feeling ugly and grumpy, I was sick of being immobile in my hospital bed. The doctors wouldn't give me crutches yet but allowed me to receive visitors. Surely Emil's visit, his first, would buoy my spirits.

"I have something for you," Emil said, as he drew close, pushing aside the mosquito netting that was gathered above my bed. He seemed happy to offer a gift, adding a kiss to my forehead before placing a copy of John Muir's *Travels in Alaska* on the bleached bedsheet. Then he took a step back to take in the full measure of my delight. He remembered how I loved reading about Muir's discoveries in California. Now Alaska. A thoughtful gift. My spirits were lifting as I'd hoped.

"Come here. I won't bite you, and I promise not to run away," I said playfully. Part of me was willing myself to be strong by acting that way.

He stepped forward and offered an odd smile. Only one side of his mouth turned upward. As he drew closer, I grabbed his hand through the netting. It had the look but not the strength I remembered.

"I know you're going to get through this. Just fine and dandy," Emil said. "Just dandy."

Gently massaging his hand, I hoped to feel something in return. I searched Emil's face, but his eyes were elsewhere and had yet to linger on mine. Maybe it was too early for visitors. I tried smiling again to show I was on the mend.

"The doctors said I was lucky. They took the leg below the knee. Take your book off the bed. I want to show it to you," I said, as I began to pull the bed sheet aside.

"Virginia. You don't need to do this."

I threw it off anyway. "Look at my stump," I said, trying to be brave.

"Below the knee. Yes. That's most fortunate, darling," Emil said without conviction. His face tightened. His body shifted, uncomfortably. But his eyes said the most. They fixed on the iron rail at the end of the bed, then moved to the ceiling. "I'm sorry. I've never been a good patient—or a good visitor," he said, smiling weakly.

I tried, but Emil's gestures, his movements and expression, seemed to confirm my worst fears. I had changed. The marshes of Gediz had turned me into something repulsive, something hideous, something unlovable for all time. I wanted to shout, *Look at me! Goddammit. It's me. I'm still Virginia!* But I kept my thoughts to myself. I was fighting the feeling, acting brave even as the wave of self-disgust and disappointment washed over me. My carefully constructed façade of sand was dissolving.

"You'll see. In a little while, you'll be back on your feet," Emil said. Then he stammered, "Your foot . . . back on . . . you know, you'll be up and about in a jiffy."

I didn't want to feel badly about myself. Not this time. It was unfair, I know, but I couldn't help it. My emotions had been piling up all day like those damn storm clouds, and I didn't care the others in the ward could hear me.

"You won't look at me. My wound. Look at it! Look at it!" I pointed to my stump. More words were caught in my throat. My face was hot. I boiled over. "Goddammit! Look at my goddam stump! My leg's gone. It's gone. It's gone!" I was shouting through tears when I said those last hurtful words: "You have no idea what I'm going through. You never will . . ."

I was ashamed by my outburst. I was lashing out at Emil, but I was furious with myself. How I hated displays of weakness. Here I was prostrate in my hospital bed, desperately wanting to regain some dignity and control over my life. Some emotional balance.

Emil seemed surprised and wounded by my outburst, and yet he moved forward to touch my hand. "I didn't mean to upset you," he said. "You know how I feel about you."

You know how I feel about you. Emil had used those same words on the beach as his hands were stroking my calves and my thighs. I didn't want to, but my mind went deeper to that day. How he'd whispered in my ear, told me how firm and strong my limbs were and how he loved them so. Then I'd used them to please him. And we cried out together.

My eyes were fixed on the jumbled hospital bedsheets and my grotesquely swollen stump. My eyes began to fill. I turned my head to the pillow.

After a few minutes, I regained my composure. "Look Emil," I said. "Neither of us expected any of this." I used my wrist to wipe my eyes. "I've been set back and need time to work this out. Reestablish myself." I told him I'd spend time in my mother's house outside of Baltimore. The place we called Box Horn Farm.

He protested, saying we could work through this together. But I told him he needed time, too, to consider his future. Would he want to be with a woman who could no longer climb the mountains he loved so dearly? Still, he wasn't ready to let me go. He said he'd take time off to help me recuperate. "Let me come with you to Maryland," he said.

I told him no. It was the anger and self-loathing speaking when I pushed him away, but underneath it all, I hoped that someday we'd be together again.

FEBRUARY 1934, MARYLAND

Box Horn in winter. It was February when I arrived back home. A crust of snow had been on the ground for weeks—too long without an enduring sun—so what remained melted then refroze, melted and refroze, each time becoming thinner and harder than the night before. And what lingered was flat and white on the gravel driveway that led up to the old farmhouse. The house itself was large and white with black shutters and a wraparound porch with gray slats. The outside was a tangle of forsythia and honeysuckle, fragrant in the spring, but that year the buds held tight.

1934 was the year the spring never came. We were desperately looking for relief—from the cold and from the Great Depression, too, that held a grip on all of us. Those were distressing times. Bread lines and soup kitchens everywhere. Though raised in an upper-middle-class household, we lost a lot in the crash, but our family was more fortunate than most. We had some money and the farm, where we raised chickens and goats, cooked our meals and took warmth from a wood burning stove. Still, my brother John had lost his job in the brick factory and left home in search of work. My own dear father, Ned, who had worked so hard to secure our position, had passed two years before. So, my mother and I were left to face that winter alone.

It was an adjustment, those early days. I hated being dependent on wheelchairs and crutches, so I spent most of the time hopping around on one leg, angry at the world, angry at my condition, but mostly angry with myself and my own stupidity. Yelling and lashing out at everything within earshot. Even the goats would look up and run to the barn when they saw me hobble down the hill to retrieve the mail. How could I have been so careless? Why hadn't I given my gun to Tod? I asked those questions over and over again, each time without one bit of satisfaction. The questions without answers are the hardest ones to face, because they come back to haunt you.

I received letters from my colleagues at State, which only made matters worse. It seemed that life was going on quite well without me. Tod and Elaine sent some of my favorite French vanilla and praline cookies, but they were mostly crumbs by the time they arrived in the shoe box with wax paper. I did enjoy the letter they penned that gave the latest gossip about who was getting promoted and reassigned the next cycle. I enjoyed it, that is, until the final line. Tod and Elaine said their two-year tour in Smyrna was up. They would be moving to Caracas in the spring. Somehow, I knew in my heart I'd never see them again. It was as if my past life was being cleaved from my body just as surely as my left leg had been.

The letters and cards from colleagues kept me thinking about my eventual return to the State Department, where I'd pick up the pieces of my career and move forward with my plan to take the Foreign Service exam. I didn't hide my ambition. Everyone knew my life's dream was to serve in the diplomatic corps.

Then one day an official-looking envelope arrived, and I tore it open, eager to see what my bosses had in store for me. Was it a new assignment? A new exotic destination? The first paragraph expressed interest in my condition in a bureaucratic kind of way. Wished me well in my recovery. Said the department would reinstate me. Give me my old job back as a clerk. But the deeper my eyes reached into the letter, the more I understood. They'd saved the letter's real purpose for the last paragraph. I dropped the paper to the ground.

"All applicants for the US Foreign Diplomatic Service must be able-bodied. An amputation of any portion of a limb, except a finger or toe, is cause for rejection. Under current regulations it would not be possible for Miss Hall to qualify for entry into the Foreign Service."

I had staked my future on joining the diplomatic corps, working my way higher to ambassador. Now it seemed, all had been lost. Furious, I protested, wrote letters, made calls, even used an old family friend with connections to take up my cause. Why couldn't I serve as a diplomat? Good God in heaven, were they afraid I couldn't dance the waltz at a diplomatic reception? The doctors hadn't cut off my head for Christ's sake.

I fought it hard and tried to remain hopeful, but another letter came, a typewritten note from Secretary of State, Cordell Hull. It read:

"Miss Hall could become a fine career girl in the Consular Service."

That was it. No explanation. No regret. Behind my back, my fate had been sealed. I would rise no higher.

So unfair. It was hard not to be bitter. Who wouldn't be? All that I had held dear—my lover, friends, career, leg—all had all been torn from me. And now I was on that blasted farm alone with my mother.

On my worst days at Box Horn, I sat outside in the cold in my wheelchair, looking up at the sun—a dull disk wrapped in a gray shroud. On my lap, I held a Winchester thirty-aught-six from my father's gun rack. In front of me, a hundred yards away, was a wooden target that had been nailed to a red oak years before. I'd shoot and shoot at that old target. I was a good shot and I got better. When an occasional squirrel or crow wandered into my sights, I didn't spare them, and I'm damn sure I killed that old oak, too.

It was my mother, Barbara, of all people, who helped me to see through the pain. I remember her in the kitchen drying the dishes one evening when she said she was fed up with my complaining. She was right when she said, "Your father and I didn't raise you to be an ill-tempered whiner." She confronted me, told me to take a deeper look at myself beyond my missing limb.

She surprised me most when she called the loss of my leg a superficial wound. "The greater wound," she said, "is the one that has pierced your soul. The wound that caused you to think of yourself as something less than whole. Something less than fully human. Something less than a complete woman. That's the wound," Mother said, "that will take the longest time to heal."

Up until that time, I'd looked past my mother, discounted her like many daughters do. Well, after she challenged me to be better than I was, I saw my mother with new eyes and our relationship deepened. I didn't always agree with her—she never did think my beaus, Emil or anyone else, were ever good enough. But I could count on her honesty. She became a mirror for me, helping me to see what lay buried deep inside. It was at Box Horn that I started the long journey to rebuild myself, to clear away the wreckage and brokenness, and to lay the foundation for the person I could become.

CHAPTER FIVE

Dindy later told her mother she saw many horrible things. As a
warning, the Nazis hung their enemies on meat hooks
in the main square.

LORNA CATLING
VIRGINIA'S NIECE

AUGUST 1941, LYON

The soldiers, smoking and laughing, lingered on the front steps of the brothel on the Rue de la Revolution, while a large-busted matron in a low-cut red print dress moved about, touching the men lightly and leaving a trail of laughter and sweet lavender perfume. Madame sauntered to the curb of the cobblestone street, lit a Gauloise and lifted her head to push out a steady stream of white. When the laughter died, I walked across the cobblestone street and casually asked for a light. She gave me the burning ember dangling from her thick red lips.

I returned it. "I hear the seafood in Lyon is excellent. Have you tried the mussels from Provence?" I said in a voice just loud enough for her to hear.

She gave me a quizzical look, as if I were a specimen in a glass jar, and she walked away.

I was coming to the surface, saying those crazy nonsensical words, and I didn't like it. Though Madame had offered no response she hadn't spurned me, so I made another approach. "Have you tried the mussels from Provence?"

Again she was silent, but looking straight ahead, cocked her head to the left toward a darkened traboule, the arched hallway that connected her establishment with a patisserie. She walked toward it slowly, and I followed a moment later.

"No," she said. "I haven't tried the mussels from Provence, but I hear the scallops are delicious." Madame Guerin twisted her head to each side then, inhaled deeply, dropped the butt, and crushed it with the ball of her foot. Smoke escaped her mouth as she spoke. "Lyon is a dangerous place," she said in a forced whisper. "Good for business, yes, but like a farmhand, I must service these filthy swine."

Madame's speech was direct and intense, like a boiler under pressure. Now the steam would be released. "Our men and food are shipped to Germany, and the women are left behind. Look around you." She nodded to the street. "The stores are empty. The panic already has set in, and in a few months? When the snows come? Starvation is next."

Madame looked toward the brothel. "This life, no one wants it, but without work we cannot live, so wives, daughters, girlfriends sell the only thing that has not been stolen from them." Guerin glanced down the alley again. "Nazis bastards. They write to Heidi to say they know the way to church, but the path to my house is well worn."

We heard boisterous laughter, so I got to the point. "I need an apartment where I can work without being disturbed. Do you have a place?"

"Yes. I was going to give it to a young man who approached me ten days ago, but he didn't say the right words, and his nervousness alarmed me. The gestapo use such men to discover Vichy's enemies. Still, there was something childlike about this young man, but I have my girls to protect, so I dismissed him as a provocateur, yes, a boy provocateur. I said I knew nothing of what he wanted and shooed him away."

A soldier walked by the alley. Again, I asked about the room.

"I have a small one near the Gare de Lyon-Part Dieu. It's not much: a bed, two chairs, a table in a bad part of town, so no one will bother you."

She pulled a metal ring with keys from inside her sizable cleavage. Quickly rummaging through the collection, Madame Guerin selected one. "Here, take this. Eighteen Rue Boileau. If you need me, I'm here on my steps at eight, bringing in customers. The morning trade is slow." Guerin looked at me and then away. "There is another man, a doctor, who treats my girls. He's helped your people, too. You'll meet, but now you must go."

Strange, I felt at home with this busty woman who smelled of burnt tobacco and cheap perfume. She reminded me of Mother. Not outwardly. Not her cloying scent or loud, oversized personality, and certainly not her garish dress—Mother was too refined for that—but Madame Guerin seemed to have an honest, no-matter-what kind of courage. The kind needed to hold families together at a time when others were falling apart.

Guerin offered a bicycle—scrapped-up, red, with fat balloon tires, fenders and a basket—and said it was the only way to get around Lyon. I hadn't ridden one since Cuthbert arrived, and over the next few days, I learned to regain my balance, pushing harder with my right hip and knee to overcome my wooden companion's lethargy. The additional effort was worth it. The bicycle, with the fresh breeze flowing through my hair, offered a kind of freedom and time to think.

As I biked through Lyon and back to the convent, my thoughts drifted to Box Horn and Mother, now alone on the farm. Before I boarded the steamer to Lisbon, I had received weekly letters, which coming so frequently, contained little real news. Reading them was like watching a flower grow. John was moving up the ladder in his new job in the ceramics factory. The garden produced a bumper crop of tomatoes this year. It looked like Maxine, our Guernsey, was going to give birth again. Nothing of great consequence, but that wasn't the point.

Fragments of life and home kept me grounded, and despite the Depression, her letters were relentlessly cheerful and offered a reminder that the world still held a place where people lived their lives without hindrance or cruelty.

Mother always wanted what was best but never pried into my work life. When I told her I was taking a new job overseas and then turned silent, she understood. She never questioned me. All she said was, "Well, I'm just going to keep sending those letters anyway, but I know you'll be too busy to write."

Of course, once I was in France, I never received her letters nor could I send any home. In my fragile world, Philomene or Germaine or Marie could never meet Virginia Hall, and my co-conspirators were not journalists or businessmen or ordinary French citizens but clandestine agents working to destroy the regime around us. And with the Germans' ruthless letter-opening and eavesdropping campaign? It was too great a risk. The only news that could arrive at Box Horn would come with two soldiers and the knock at the door.

That night I lay awake thinking about Albert. How we were surrounded by a world of hatred and repression, where the Gestapo and round-ups and ghostly lives existed together in a scorched world of despair. Usually, I'm able to suppress the loneliness and ugliness of life, but that night the evil couldn't be pushed away. I tried hard to create a small space in my mind where pleasurable thoughts of home and my earlier, less complicated life could take root.

In thinking about my mother and Box Horn that day, I had opened the door to a dusty room that had not seen light for years. My body had healed the best it could, and the wound my mother said had pierced my spirit had mended, too. And now as thoughts of Box Horn blossomed, I let my mind wander.

Emil came to mind. My blood surged.

In my self-centeredness, I had not kept in contact, and now I was inconsequential to his life. People drift from each other in war. That's what I told myself. But I didn't want to think of France or Turkey or Poland, or where Emil might be in that tangled mess. Tonight, I didn't care. I needed him in my imagination.

Emil, with his black hair curled back in a small wave behind his ears, with the sweet scent of sandalwood and clove, and his strong carpenter hands. My memories caused my skin to flush. Here I was, in a convent, lying on a stiff monastic bed with a single sheet and horsehair blanket. I was a tortured being stretched on an inquisitor's rack. But under the eyes of an enormous crucifix, the impious thoughts had already arrived, and I couldn't suppress them. I gave in, freed myself, and my bonds slipped away.

I thought of Emil's back. I remembered its V-shaped flair like some untamed jungle beast. My hands stroked the ridges of his spine where the cords stiffened and relaxed with a quickening pace, and in the morning, his arms and legs entwined with mine.

So I lifted the hem of my plain cotton nightgown and began with a tentative touch to remember Emil's strong hands and how he used his mouth. Then, using my fingers, I traced the movement of his tongue on the lobe of my ear, moving slowly down the curve of my neck, then lower still. Then I began to explore the secret spot he knew so well. In my mind, he was with me in the mountains facing a warm wind; then on the sand as the waves washed over us; then I was on top, looking directly at Emil, each movement of my hips causing his eyes to tighten and release with pleasure. Soon, the river overflowed its banks, the dam burst, and all the ugliness, hatred, and despair that surrounded me were swept away. The pillow muffled my cry.

As my heart returned to a slower beat, I remembered the brooch in the zippered compartment of my purse and thought of Emil and where he might be.

Perhaps in war, I needed something to hold onto, someone to believe in, someone who cared for me in a special way. Once that person had been Emil. Maybe it could be again. In the coming days, I kept my brooch close, and I began to touch my watch, too. Though we couldn't share space, we could share time, and while I didn't know where Emil was or what he was doing, he might be thinking of me at the very instant I was thinking of him. And if only for a moment, we might be joined.

That was the last night I spent in the convent.

*   *   *

Madame was right. Rue Boileau was in a horrible section of Lyon, remarkable for its urban landscape of dereliction: piles of garbage and debris, splintered glass, decrepit buildings of wood and stone. The safe house Guerin offered was decaying and spare but clean—a two room walk-up with a sturdy single bed, a table and two chairs, just as she had said, and all in satisfactory condition. The rooms' white walls, stained brown, emitted a musty odor, and spots of black mold spotted the ceiling. All of it, as unpleasant as it was, was not disqualifying. On the contrary, I loved the apartment, so close to the train station and shielded from gestapo eyes. Madame's a-pied de terre, hidden amid the rubble, was just right for clandestine meetings.

I wouldn't reside in this safe house. I needed separate accommodations to live my journalist cover, and I began my search on the streets of Lyon, filled with refugees who seemed to mill about, listlessly, without hope. I was fortunate, but even with a surplus of francs, it took a full day to find the right accommodations. Cuthbert complained bitterly about my endless march up and down the cobblestone streets, but it all turned out for the best when I found a comfortable new apartment for us on Rue Grolle. Le Grand Nouvelle met my requirements—a bar on the ground floor for interviews, an upper-floor apartment with a front window from which I could observe the gestapo's Black Marias move about the main street, and a convenient backdoor to the alley for a quick departure.

I settled in quickly and began recording my observations as any journalist would. The leaves on the plane trees were turning, and there was bite to the morning air. The killing frost was on its way, and soon the wind from the north would turn the ground to stone. With the seasons turning colder, I sensed a growing anxiety. The competition for fuel and food had begun to play out in the shops. Even the wilted vegetables, pathetic cuts of meat, and gaunt-looking hens were gone from the shelves and from behind glass cases.

Everyone complained terribly of being squeezed. If it wasn't the Nazis stealing the best produce and shipping it to Deutschland, it was the greedy farmers withholding their crops to extort the best black market prices. Everyone was on edge. The word on the street? There wouldn't be enough to go around. Starvation would visit Lyon.

Famine. At first it was only whispered, but the shadowy specter of gaunt bodies wasting away lingered in the imagination and in the vacant eyes of the living. The cruel vision of loved ones hungry and cold—would it unleash passions that might lead to desperate acts, riots, looting, even assassinations, actions no one would have considered before?

I couldn't alter their predicament. My job was to report on it. The how of it all. How might the people respond? How might the British intelligence harness these primal passions to drive a wedge between the people and the Vichy government? Meanwhile, that scoundrel Prime Minister Pierre Leval and his appalling Vichy cronies were keeping themselves above it all by pitting their countrymen against each other, using shameful claims that their sad state was the fault of the Jews. The pressure on the people of Lyon was mounting from all quarters. That much I knew.

Without my pianist, Albert, my messages went through Western Union to my cutout, George Backer, at the *New York Evening Post*. The paragraphs about food shortages and growing discontent were in clear text, but news that Albert was burned and missing was sent in code.

And then I broke the rules. There was more to my message, a special request. Official channels shouldn't be used for personal reasons, but I didn't care. It was about Emil. He had re-entered my life, if only in my mind, and I had to know where he was, that he was all right. So, I told SOE to check their files, track down any information they might have on Lt. Emil Stanisz of the Polish Army. His last known location: Smyrna, Turkey. That was sent in code too.

The next few days were devoted to housekeeping, mostly establishing the routine expected of a journalist, and bicycling the uneven cobblestone streets of Lyon to get reacquainted with the city and people. I spoke with neighbors at Le Grand Nouvelle to make myself known and gain their trust, and followed up with Wittinghill, too, who said he had several contacts for me to interview. He made appointments for the following week.

With Albert dangling precariously somewhere in Lyon, I made a point to call on Madame Guerin and returned to the Rue de la Revolution with hopes she might have more news about the young man she'd dismissed. She was on the steps of her establishment, just after eight, smoking a cigarette with a customer. Our eyes met, and she motioned me to the rear courtyard.

It was the last mild day of the season, and the swallowtails were circling the lavender and purple coneflowers of her unkempt country garden. She arrived a few moments later. I got to the point: the boy provocateur.

"Collette told me about one of her clients," said Guerin, "a gestapo officer named Schmidt—a big, powerful man with arms like tree trunks, who likes to be disciplined for his naughty ways. He confesses his sins so Collette will use the whip. Fortunate for us," Guerin said nodding slightly, "this Schmidt has a big mouth to match his big ass.

"Schmidt said this boy, Albert, squealed like a pig. It was surprising how boastful he was talking of such horrible things. We have rough customers but none so cold-hearted." Guerin asked if I wanted to speak with Colette.

The circle had to stay closed. I declined and asked Guerin to tell me as much as she could remember.

Guerin told me Albert claimed to be a businessman named Speer from Brussels, a supplier of ammunition for the Germans, in Lyon looking for conscripts for his factory. But his story didn't hold up. His *carte d'identitè* was crudely made, she said, dark blue ink was used instead of black. Worst of all, Albert was caught in a café lavatory with a suitcase containing his wireless equipment.

Guerin said, "This new Gestapo Chief, Barbie. Klaus Barbie is a monster. Albert was taken to Barbie's basement chamber. Barbie said, 'You are from England, and you are what they call a pianist. You should know that I play several instruments, too.' And then Barbie pointed to terrible tools on his cart with wheels. One of them was an iron bar.

"Barbie gave this boy a choice. He said, 'You can be shot as a spy now, or we can play these instruments together.' He gave the boy another option. He said, 'Work for us and live.' Albert refused. Schmidt laughed when he said the bar was brought down with such force that the boy's fingers showed the form of the bar."

"After Barbie started using the scalpel," Guerin said, "Albert broke down and gave up his true name. And then . . . the name of his contact in Lyon."

My back stiffened.

Guerin continued. "He was supposed to meet a woman, Agent 3844, in Lyon. Then Albert said, 'You can kill me but I have no more information.' Barbie said, 'I believe you,' and gave the order to Schmidt. 'Give the boy his wish, and hang him in the square.'"

Guerin looked down. "Before Barbie finished, Albert gave up one last piece of information. This Agent 3844," Guerin said, "is *la dame qui boite*. The lady who limps."

CHAPTER SIX

---

*Many families are divided brutally, part living on one side of the
demarcation line, part on the other, with no communication. And many
sons, brothers, fathers, and fiancés are still prisoners in Germany. People
separated from those they love are living under constant mental strain.*

VIRGINIA HALL
NEW YORK EVENING POST

SEPTEMBER 1941, LYON

My first thought was Alesh. The secret police. They'd pay him a visit, so I had Guerin ask one of her girls to arrange a meeting. That same day Madame returned with news: the abbe was nowhere to be found.

Life's complexity reached a new level. Two days. That's what they told us at Beaulieu. After capture, hold out for two days. If you must, scream freely but speak through gritted teeth. That's what it takes for your agents to cover their tracks: move to a new safe house, change names, make their escape. Now, who else did Albert give to Barbie? Guerin had sent him away, and thank God, my tracks were light. I'd never met Albert in Beaulieu, where I was known by the number, 3844. The gestapo had just one dot, one point, a woman with a limp, but by now I was certain word had spread. The chase was on.

Albert's brutal death, my first encounter with pure evil, fed my paranoia and obsession with security. After Guerin said Albert's forged documents had tripped had him up, I'd patted my pocket, searching for my credentials as if I were the guilty party. It was a thoughtless, stupid act that betrayed my cover as a journalist and reflected an appalling lapse in discipline.

Safely back in my hotel, I began to retrieve my several *carte d'identitè,* placed in envelopes hidden throughout the room: one wedged behind a stained mirror framed in oak, another behind a bucolic picture of longhorn cattle grazing beside a lazy river, and one more taped beneath a sliding dresser drawer. Each bore a different name known only to London. I exhaled deeply. No blue ink, each in a different handwriting. Only one with me at a time. If caught with two cards? A chill rushed up my spine.

*   *   *

I spent the next few days traveling the outskirts of Lyon, living my cover, using my *New York Post* credentials, asking questions while keeping an ear to the ground about where the abbe might be. Was he hiding? Had he been picked up? My observations were turned into stories for *the Post* of how the war had transformed the towns of Vichy and Lyon. What Nazi rule and Vichy government acquiescence had done to these once vibrant cities. How the country had been divided into occupied and unoccupied zones. The millions of French citizens in German labor camps and how these cruel policies separated families, creating feelings of loneliness and longing.

"Free France" was the name the Vichy government had given to the interior zone not occupied by the German military, a name the Vichy clung to without any sense of irony. Of course, there was no such thing as "Free France," nothing of the sort. Vichy was a fig leaf that couldn't cover the naked truth of German domination. And now, the tide of refugees rushing into Vichy after Paris fell had turned the new capital infinitesimally small. It had become a metaphor for French pride, I think, assaulted, conquered, diminished.

Vichy, once a special little town on a river, now was no different from the others. The fear of starvation had taken hold, and the essentials—bread, lard, and what little meat available—were all restricted. Lives once filled with pride and purpose now had been reduced to snipping little coupons from ration books: ten ounces of bread a day; two ounces of cheese a week; six ounces a month of what passed for coffee. The small pleasures of life had disappeared too. Grown men and women scurried to pick up cigarette butts tossed to the street by laughing German soldiers. Only French men had the privilege of an occasional Gauloise. No cigarette ration for women. And wine? The lifeblood of France was almost nonexistent. The police even controlled the purchase of bicycle tires and inner tubes.

I bicycled everywhere—there was no real private transportation save the Black Marias, the large official cars with oversized fenders that ferried the gestapo, French secret police, and Vichy officials around town. The public busses that spewed black smoke were always crowded and though Cuthbert complained bitterly, I told him the bicycle was good for us. He was put to the test, pushing that left pedal thousands of times each day.

My seemingly innocent rides that stretched for miles into the countryside north and east of Lyon had a more serious intent. I was searching for remote landing and drop zones, where the single engine Lizzies—the matte black Lysanders that held a pilot plus two—could land or drop supplies. London gave us exacting specifications for landings—at least six hundred by twelve hundred yards of a flat, treeless terrain serviced by a road, and away from gestapo and police eyes.

The flood plains adjacent to the river Saone, north toward St. Cyr and east on the Rhone, seemed ideal, and I dutifully recorded the best spots, giving each a code name—Artichoke, Lucky Strike, Pluto—and offered directions using railroad tracks, mountains, and tributaries as reference points. My reports were sent to London in coded letters, and I then turned to recruiting a reception committee. When the time was right we would meet these flights on nights when the moon was full. We'd carry torches to guide the pilots to the drop zone, and when the silk parachutes fluttered to the ground, we'd collect the leather cylinders containing weapons, equipment, money and some simple pleasures—like soap, chocolate, a jar of Noxzema for Cuthbert, and we'd distribute what we collected to the waiting citizen-soldiers. But the day of drops and landings had not yet arrived. We were planning, readying ourselves for operations that would liberate France.

*   *   *

It was a blustery Monday at the beginning of September when I arrived at the Café de la Revolution in Vichy to meet Vice Consul Wittinghill's contact, the government's minister of information, Paul Marion. I ordered coffee, dutifully clipped a coupon from my forged ration book, and waited patiently under a tattered red umbrella for Marion to arrive. A few minutes later a Black Maria rolled up and disgorged a man, impeccably dressed in a dark suit and pushed-back hair, and a fashionably dressed young woman wearing red lipstick and a black and white checked print dress.

I rose to meet Marion, extended my right hand, and with my left, opened and lifted the thin wallet that held my press credentials.

He took my hand without firmness and nodded at my papers. Yes, everything was in order. Marion introduced his protégé, chief censor Suzanne Bertillon. Both accepted my card.

"So tell me," I said, sipping my coffee, seated directly across from Marion. "I was in Vichy and Lyon back in the thirties before the war, so I know how things were. It must be hard for people to accept their new station—ration cards, no petrol, men being requisitioned to work in Germany. My readers of the *New York Evening Post* want to know. How are the people of this region holding up?"

"First," said Marion, "let me say . . . let me tell your readers that as a former journalist, I know what beats in the heart of all Frenchmen. We long for peace and stability. The French people are strong. It could be much worse, but the Germans assure us that it won't be long now, and our lives will return to normal. We're optimistic that the situation will turn around very soon, nevertheless we must . . ."

As Marion droned on, his young assistant, Bertillon, a stylish woman with chin-length chestnut hair, a pale complexion, and delicate features, was shifting in her seat. She had a pained expression, and she looked away. It appeared difficult for her to hear this story yet again.

"But of course," Marion continued, "there are threats to the people of this region. Spies have started entering the Haute Loire. This was not unexpected, but it is a new development. The brave people of Vichy need to be vigilant—guard against outsiders from upsetting the calm we have tried so hard to create. We are under difficult circumstances, yes, but we are making the best with what we have. Agitators are trying to upset our relationship with the Germans."

Bertillon turned toward me and for a moment, our eyes met. We smiled. I tried to conceal my boredom, but the young protégé had to know I wasn't buying Marion's platitudes. He didn't seem to notice our connection.

"If you don't mind me interrupting, Mr. Minister," I said, "What evidence do you have to say outsiders are entering Vichy?"

"Why, a few days ago, the gestapo gave me information for a bulletin we just posted about a spy they picked up in a cafe on the streets of Lyon," he said. "Think of it. A British agent here in Lyon! How he got here is anyone's guess. Perhaps," Marion pointed upward, "he dropped from the stars. God only knows. I don't get involved with police matters. The gestapo says they expect more foreigners to infiltrate Free France, so we need to remain on guard. We have begun to offer rewards for information on Frenchmen or foreigners who try to upset our way of life."

I looked up from the notes I was taking. "I can understand your desire for calm, but what else can you tell my readers about those who threaten it?"

"We have constructive relations with the American vice consul in Lyon." A look of disdain crossed his face. "But we have less cooperation, far less, with your embassy in Vichy. America is neutral in this war, and some neutral embassies and consulates are anything but impartial. We suspect several are supporting British interests, and—who knows—maybe its secret agents. So you can see, the threats to our way of life come from many directions—from our own misguided citizens, foreign spies, and governments purporting to be evenhanded."

"Why do you say the threats are increasing? And what about that British spy?" I asked with a touch of playfulness, putting my pencil down. "If you prefer, this can be off the record. I don't need to quote you directly or even place what you say in the paper."

"I'm afraid I have nothing more to add. I've said too much already," Marion said with a sniff.

"They say there's another agent, a Canadian woman in Lyon," Bertillon blurted.

"Miss Bertillon," Marion said with a scowl, "that is quite enough. We don't want to confuse Miss Hall with unconfirmed rumor. That's off the record, Miss Hall."

"Yes. Of course," I said, acting to control my nerves. "But a woman, you say. That is so interesting, so unique. A Mati Hari no doubt, seducing Vichy officials? I can understand the minister's interest in keeping this hush-hush, but there must be just a bit more you can add—not for the paper," I said with warmth, "but on background?"

"Nothing more," said Marion. "And if you'll excuse us, it's time to leave. Remember. That's off the record, Miss Hall. It's strictly hearsay. Come along, Miss Bertillon. We must get back to the ministry."

Marion grabbed his assistant's elbow and hurried her back to the Black Maria waiting by the curb. Bertillon glanced at me over her left shoulder just before the door slammed shut.

I stayed behind to drink my coffee; I'd only taken a few sips. A Canadian woman? A fortunate blunder. As I reached for my purse to pay the bill, my hand knocked over the cup, spilling the liquid across the table.

The gestapo was collecting information on me—from Albert's interrogation no doubt, and from someone close to me. The priest? Where was he? If he didn't surface soon, I'd have to assume he'd been burned and what he knew about me given up. One thing seemed certain. My freedom depended on information, fresh sources of information.

I liked Bertillon's verve, and it seemed she was fed up with the lies being spewed by Marion and the ministry. She was in a useful position too. As chief censor, she read intercepted mail, knew who Vichy was watching, and how secrets might slip through government hands undetected.

The thought occurred to me just as our eyes met. Bertillon could be turned and become one of my reporting agents. Even before the door to the Black Maria slammed shut, I was plotting my approach. Still, as much as she probably detested the ministry, she'd be most useful working in place, feeding me the latest information from inside the ministry. All she needed was a little push.

Two days later, before I could reach out to her, Bertillon contacted me to seek advice on breaking into the newspaper business. She said she was through with the lies and had finally made her feelings known to her boss. In a fit of anger, she had quit the information ministry.

Naturally, I consoled Bertillon on her loss of employment, told her I admired her courage. "But how will you get along without income?" I asked. "The winter is coming." Then I prodded her gently to seek reinstatement, said she'd been too harsh and could make amends. A bottle of hard to find Bordeaux and a heart-felt apology might ease her return.

But my plans were for naught. It seems harsh words were spoken that couldn't be retrieved, and her departure was by mutual agreement. I was disappointed but landed on my feet, dangling the possibility of her working directly for me. She still had much to offer: a rolodex of contacts, knowledge of people under suspicion, the techniques of telephone eavesdropping and mail tampering. Would it be a difficult sell? I didn't think so.

I told her if she became my research assistant for the *New York Post* she'd use her skills to speak the truth in a free press and receive a stipend, too. It wasn't the money, though, Lord knows, she had none. It was revenge that brought Bertillon under my wing. Her hatred of Marion and her disgust with the Vichy regime. Vengeance would lead her spill all she knew and cause her to dig deeply into her rolodex of contacts. All of it would be turned over to London, to hurt the bastards destroying her country. A smart agent with access to important people and information—just the kind of recruit Buck and Vera back in London loved. A prize addition to my stable of spies in

Heckler. Then I closed the deal:

"What could be a better fit? A former information officer working for a newspaper?"

She beamed and said yes.

But I had a concern—her temper. I understood the fire that builds inside at seeing the injustice all around, when people are denied their basic right to live in peace. Buck had claimed that my own emotions could land me in trouble someday too, so I understood Bertillon's passion, which could be too strong for her own good.

For Bertillon's protection and my own, I'd reveal only what she needed to know and keep her separate from my other agents. I was known to her as Virginia Hall, newswoman—no other names or identities. I gave her questions from London and told her to use her contacts, and report the facts back to me.

Security was foremost in my mind, so I met infrequently with Bertillon and then not at all. Her instructions, pay, and even her reports to me were passed between us through a series of letter boxes in the Haute Loire.

Bertillon didn't disappoint. She would become my greatest recruit—bright, productive, motivated. And when London needed more information on German and Vichy plans in Marseilles, I moved Bertillon to that dangerous port city and gave her a codename, Christine 25.

*　　*　　*

Though my newest recruit had only begun a steady stream of reporting, I was impatient with Heckler's progress. I'd turned my ear to the streets of Lyon and Vichy, and started building an intelligence network by enlisting the support of trusted contacts who could help.

But with growth comes danger. That the abbe had been missing for over a week still troubled me, and I shared my concerns with London and sought their help. SOE counterespionage had no new information. "Be careful." That's all they said, which was no help at all.

*　　*　　*

My spirits lifted the next evening when Madame Guerin asked

me to dinner in the back room of the Cafe Lion d' Or. She'd promised to introduce her doctor friend, a potential recruit. Heckler could use a doctor's services and a fresh letterbox.

Heavy shades and garish purple velvet wallpaper darkened the space jammed with small tables. Seated beside Madame was a bespectacled man with a shiny pate, who stood when I entered. He nodded slightly as a courtesy, but he didn't say a word.

"This is the doctor I told you about," Guerin said with eager eyes. "Marie, I'd like you to meet Doctor Rousset."

I extended my hand and chose an anodyne greeting, one that any acquaintance of a friend might offer. I played the role of a kindly woman, milquetoast, I suppose, without any edge at all, to dispel the notion that I was observing the doctor—which of course I was. Very closely. I looked for any stray, signs—hesitation in speech, awkward movement of his head, undue sweating of his hands or beneath his nose. But mostly I looked at eyes and never trusted anyone whose orbs stayed fixed or shifted unnecessarily.

Doctor Rousset grasped my hand a bit weakly but without any hesitation or noticeable moisture. All appeared normal, but I remained wary. As my network of agents grew, Buck's departing words took on new meaning: with twelve, always an Iscariot.

"The British officer, Simpson, was in dreadful shape before we got him to the good doctor," said Madame.

"Madame Guerin is too kind," said Doctor Rousset. "Yes, the lieutenant was badly burned when his plane crashed, and he was under our care for several months. But I find in the most severe cases that the will to live determines patient outcome. Flight Lieutenant Simpson had a strong life force. All I did was stabilize him and provide a foothold to lift himself up. He did the rest. And now I'm told he's safe in his homeland."

Doctor Rousset, well-groomed and meticulous in his black bowtie, had an open face and a triangular head larger than proportionate for his small stature. I thought it strange that his hair was gray, and yet his mustache was black, trimmed precisely to fit the corners of his upper lip. His expressive and bushy eyebrows rose and fell as he spoke, which revealed an intensity roiling beneath his mild demeanor.

As Madame Guerin passed around the menu, she recalled other pilots and soldiers Doctor Rousset had helped.

"Okay," I asked, acting the smart aleck. "What's *really* on this menu? Lamb, rosé from Provence, green beans? Are you playing a trick on us? With all the shortages, none of this has been seen in Lyon for months."

"Marie, I'm surprised. I do have some influence," Madame said in a playful, mocking tone. "This is my favorite *'restaurant noir.'* My girls and I receive some favors from the Germans: cigarettes, wine— difficult to find rationed items—and we distribute them to friends— like Henri, the owner of this restaurant. In return, I bring some friends here on occasion. It's like a lot of things in France these days; there are marriages for love and marriages of convenience."

As glasses were filled a second time, our conversation turned more animated and the doctor's tongue loosened. Our talk turned to events of the day.

The vein just above the bridge of Rousset's nose had begun to swell.

"What the gestapo did in Chalon-sur-Rhone was unspeakable," he said. "One German sergeant stabbed. Fifty people . . . fifty innocents machine gunned in the back." As the doctor spoke, a small spittle flew from his mouth. His eyes narrowed. "And dumped into a shallow grave before relatives could claim their bodies. That makes a French- man's blood boil." The doctor finished the last spot of red in his glass.

I interjected calmly, "Some would disagree with the stabbing, because it led to retaliation. In my job as a reporter, I hear things. People say that when the time is right, action against the Germans must be planned and executed without passion. Pockets of resistance are beginning to form all over France. Some are Polish or Czech groups with people who can't go home, so they fight the Germans where they can, in France."

"And the Communists," Guerin added, "were betrayed by the Germans. They fight the Nazis with vigor."

"I support de Gaulle," Doctor Rousset said raising his voice. "The general will return to liberate France."

I gave a small nod in support of these overly optimistic sentiments.

"But each of these groups is isolated and without a plan," I said. "Without plans, without coordination, Germans will destroy each resistance group, one by one."

Without revealing too much, I said there were people overseas that could help, but they would need the support of patriotic Frenchmen and Frenchwomen.

"It is hard to work with others overseas," Doctor Rousset said, looking away. "Especially, with the British. Our history with them is not good."

I shrugged. "But as Madame Guerin said, there are marriages of love and marriages of convenience. When the time is right, the French must accept help from beyond their borders to expel the Germans. My publisher tells me the British are coordinating their plans with de Gaulle across the channel."

"Well, then I can support this." Doctor Rousset, cooling, gave a small nod.

We'd said enough for one evening, our meal was over, but I had a last thought for the group.

"A newspaper would cease to exist without protecting the confidentiality of its sources. For our safety, each of us should agree not to repeat the conversations of this night."

Before leaving, I took the doctor aside and told him I needed a letterbox for sending my stories back to the *Post*. He volunteered one in his office then said softly that he knew others who could help: Madame Catin—who later would serve as my courier in Le Puy; Madame and Monsieur Labourier, who managed a fleet of trucks; and a husband and wife team who owned a printing press. I thanked the doctor and told him to stay silent until I had a chance to meet them.

It was a heady but dangerous time. My organization, Heckler, was growing, but who could I trust? Alesh? Where was he?

CHAPTER SEVEN

---

*The Abbe did not make a very favorable impression on me and
I wired London giving his name and address, asking that he be
checked by (intelligence) agents in Paris. I wanted instructions
on what to do with him.*

*London, in reply, said to continue to take his stuff . . . and give him
one hundred thousand francs and film for microphoto work.*

VIRGINIA HALL

OCTOBER 1941, LYON

My questions about the abbe's whereabouts were soon
answered. Guerin met the sexton, Barthelme, sweeping
the stone steps leading to the church. He said the abbe
had returned.

Not knowing if the priest was being watched, my unannounced
visit during confession seemed a risky move but I had too many
questions. The most important being: could the priest be trusted? I
took precautions, walking slowly by the monastery—its arched glass
windows iridescent red and yellow in the bright sun—past empty
shops and stale patisserie, before tracking back to the chapel. Clean
of tails. Only two elderly women, stooped and clothed in long black
dresses, were making their way slowly up the stairs to the dark oak
doors of the ancient stone building.

I entered through the side door and was plunged into a blinding dark. My left hand worked the wall of confessional booths tentatively, as Cuthbert slid along the smooth marble floor. From behind an open door I heard labored breathing and a long sigh. The silhouette of the abbe was visible through the wood lattice separating our compartments. My blindness lifted.

"I've missed you," I said calmly, pulling the door shut with a soft click.

The priest took out a tattered cloth and swabbed his forehead, bowed to the ground. He sniffed. His eyes stayed fixed.

"I read the notice on the wooden post at Place Bellecour," he said nervously. "About the British agent. Albert . . . the man the gestapo hunted and tortured. I saw his broken body, hung in the square for the crows and vermin to devour."

The abbe lowered his voice. "I was frightened. So frightened. I am a man of faith taught to put my trust in God, but I confess when my moments of doubt are so great, I take refuge in the communion wine." His bald head glistened. He dabbed the back of his neck, and placed his head in his hands. "I waited. Trembling. Thinking I would share the fate of Albert." He sniffled. "I knew they would come. And they did."

I let the silence linger.

After composing himself, the abbe continued, "I am weaker than most. That I know. I lied to save myself. I said, 'A stranger knocked on my door,' and then I hid behind the Word. It says, 'Knock and the door will be opened to you.' So, I told the secret police, 'What priest would not do the same as the good Book commands? Would the Christ not open the door? Yes, as a man of God, I let him in, not for refuge but for prayer.'"

Alesh lifted his head, and in the backlight I saw his eyes were full. They returned to the ground. "I cried out, 'I am loyal to Marshall Petain and France.' They believed me and departed." He shrugged and his voice lifted. "As you can see, I am still here. Who knows the inner mind of such men? Praise God it was the police and not the gestapo. The police are cowards whose anger is rooted in humiliation. Losing their country so quickly to the Germans, and now they turn the rage of their shame loose on their own people. What Frenchman wants to throw a Catholic priest in jail? But the gestapo?" He paused and gave a wry snuffle. "They have no such prohibition, even when it comes to torture."

"Did the police question you about others you've helped?" I asked calmly.

"Yes," and then quickly added, "but I said nothing. Nothing."

"Nothing about Lucas?"

"Nothing."

I gave him more time to think before I asked my next question. The one he must have known was coming. "Did they ask about a lady with a limp?"

The Abbe hesitated. "Yes. But I would never betray . . . never reveal such a thing."

I turned silent again, waiting patiently for Alesh, who now seemed comfortable with the quiet. The priest exhaled and took his time before speaking. "But the gestapo knows you are here in the Haute Loire."

Again, I waited, but the priest had nothing more. So I asked, "And where were you these past days?"

"After the police left, I departed the abbey." He waved his hand loosely in front of his face. "I have a flock to tend. I met parishioners outside of town and in Paris. Some are too old or scared to travel, so I share the body and blood in their homes."

Did I believe the priest? I couldn't say, not yet, but the secret police wouldn't be through with him. He'd be observed, tailed, brought in for more questions. Meetings with trusted agents were risky, but now the danger was too great for me to see Alesh again. Ever. Future contact would be through cutouts and letterboxes. Guerin would have to keep her girls away from the abbe too. The priest was damaged goods.

Back in my empty hotel room, I reclined on my too soft bed. The Grand Nouvelle, earlier one of Lyon's finest, had become like all the rest: overused, tired, neglected. The pink flowered paper had begun to separate from the wall, the Oriental rug under my bed was tattered at the fringe, and there was a rust-stained, free-standing mirror leaning against the wall next to the dresser.

Cuthbert had been a pain for weeks but that night he was complaining more loudly than usual. The daily walks along the uneven cobblestone streets, miles of pushing on a bicycle pedal, and the stress of standing all day was taking its toll. His revenge was plain to see in the stained mirror. My pink stump was moist and puffy, and blisters, soft like pillows, had formed on the outer edge.

"Goddammit, Cuthbert," I muttered softly. "I pushed you hard, and you hadn't received much rest, but Christ, buck it up. There's a job to do."

I took a deep breath, exhaled slowly, and began to clean and massage my stump. That satisfied me for now. But then a thought took hold. Everyone has a breaking point, and I was sure that somewhere, sometime, Cuthbert would test mine.

But had the man of God reached his limit? Become a Judas ready to sell out Heckler for pieces of silver? The chase was underway for *la dame qui boite,* but perhaps for my co-conspirators, too. I'd press London counterespionage hard for an answer.

And what if the Abbe was clean? I shook my head. Lyon still would be too hot for the priest. He'd have to leave town now, if not for his safety then ours. Let the authorities focus on others for a while and lose interest. In the meantime, I'd give Alesh a small job, a test, to get him out of Lyon: courier information to Lucas in Paris. If he passed the test, then in time, and after he cooled off, maybe he could return.

Questions for London counterespionage, CE, were too sensitive and urgent for my cutout, George Backer at the *Post.* For this, I needed a pianist, and the closest one was in Lucas's circuit, Autogiro, southwest of Paris. Alesh would be my courier.

On a small piece of tissue paper, I wrote a coded message that told of Albert's death and queried CE again about the priest. Then I folded the paper lengthwise twice and inserted it into the barrel of a fountain pen and gave it to Alesh. We'd see if Lucas received the message.

*   *   *

A couple weeks later, I was finishing a report at Guerin's safe house when I heard a familiar signal: two hard knocks at the door followed by a light one. I'd learned through the consulate's letterbox that Major

Jacques de Guelis, head of French operations for SOE London, was to pay a visit. I was glad to see a familiar face.

"Marie," he said. "Damn good to see you. How you getting along?" The major, though in civilian clothes, was like many military men of his rank, ramrod straight and full of bluster. He entered the room with crisp precision and didn't wait for my reply. "Got your message. Bloody shame about Albert."

His tweed coat, well-made but appropriately worn, lay across his arm. I took it and pointed to the wooden table where a half bottle of Grenache, a wedge of St. Nectaire, and a baguette were waiting. We sat, and I poured the major a full glass. I didn't add detail to Albert's story or contradict his assessment.

Major de Guelis didn't seem to think Albert's capture and death would have an impact on my work. "Still, it's a lesson for us all—sound security practices," he said.

No doubt SOE had seen this story before, and now it was time to find the meaning of Albert's short existence. A single sentence with a moral hook. But the major's shallow summation was undeniable. The need for tighter personal security. I nodded in agreement.

"And your Catholic priest," he continued. "I checked with military intelligence, MI-6. The Gaullist is their agent. Novel. An asset who can live his cover. I wish we had more like him. He's clean. Use him."

"Are you sure? He was picked up by the secret police and went missing for a more than a week."

"Listen, Marie," the major said, sounding agitated. "You'll learn that agents get picked up and questioned. That's life, and MI-6 says he's clean. No derogatory information. That's what I'm told. Now, what makes you think he might be compromised?"

"His actions more than what he said. He acted suspiciously. It was his gestures, his nervous fiddling, his sweating. All of it."

"Look, he's a man of the cloth for Christ's sake and has a good track record. We'll need more to go on than a woman's intuition."

The heat rose. I'm certain the red in my face was unmistakable and my eyes surely must have been blazing orbs. I can stay cool when it counts, especially in the field, but this was different, coming from one of my own. "That intuition, major, is keeping me alive," I said, focused squarely on his eyes. "I can bear a lot of things, but not . . . It's my neck out here. Try to save it for me, will you?"

The major's face tightened. "Yes, yes, of course. I wasn't disagreeing . . ." He didn't finish the thought. Staring into his grenache, the major assured me that he would keep an ear to MI-6 counterespionage and tell me if anything new on the priest came up.

My anger seemed to have sidetracked his thoughts, but then he straightened up and said, "Let's get back to business, Heckler, shall we?" He still seemed chastened but pleased, no doubt, to change the subject and follow the unpleasantness with some compliments from London.

"You're expanding Heckler's network," he said. "You've found safe houses, food, and medical assistance for pilots and agents, and your protégé, Christine 25—most impressive. Getting yourself out of the loop; having Spanish *passeurs* bring her reports over the Pyrenees. Very smart."

I broke in to tell the major about other agents in my stable: one had access to a government press for high quality forgeries—ration cards and identity documents; another owned trucks for aircraft receptions. "But I'm still light on couriers," I said, "and I'm forming a reception committee for the Lysander drops, whenever they begin." Then I added, "I do have a few of Lyon's finest in my stable, from the gendarmerie, who have a taste for Gauloise and Chateauneuf-du-Pape."

"Good," de Guelis replied, forming a small smile. "Keep working on it. And yes, you're going to have company soon. More resident agents and military trainers. We're starting a new phase: sabotage instruction and operations. We'll be turning up the heat on the Jerrys."

As he paused, I could see the wheels turning, and what remained on his list came out rapid fire. "This is where you come in. Five agents—mission Corsican—will be dropped by Lysander aircraft this month in the occupied zone near Bergerac, and two more will land north of Perpignan by trawler, the *S.S. Fidelity*. Lucas, in the Occupied Zone, will form the reception committee for the Lizzy. The five he picks up will be operating near Paris.

"Alain and Olive from the *Fidelity* will be attached to you here in Lyon, and once the smoke settles, we'll move Olive to start a new circuit, Urchin in Marseilles. Alain will be a military trainer home-based not far from you in Lyon. Get to know him. He can help in a pinch.

"So," Major de Guelis said, his voice rising, "you will be, as they say in the States, a regular Grand Central Station soon enough. We'll be calling on you to lend a hand—lodging, food, that sort of thing, and more if things get sticky. Jerry always seem to know when we're coming, so there's the possibility of a twisted wicket."

He wasn't waiting for a response. He'd already segued to a different topic, though his voice softened and seemed to relax. "Buck and Vera send their regards and asked me to convey their thanks for the work, the splendid work, you're doing in the Haute Loire. I know they said you'd only be in France for a few months, but with all that's happening now, and . . . no pressure. Say the word and we'll bring you out. But I'm afraid you've already become indispensable. You're making a bloody good show of it. This whole endeavour . . . and, well, all of us—Buck, Vera, and the rest—we want you to stay a bit longer." He lingered on the word, "longer," which made it sound like an open-ended request. "Don't tell me now," he said. "Think it over."

Before I had a chance to say anything, the major stood and made his way to his coat, slung over a chair by the door. "Oh yes," he said. "One more thing. We received your message asking about Lt. Stansz. Emil, I think his name was. Yes, well. Any particular reason for asking?"

It was the way he said the word *was*. Something had gone terribly wrong. "An acquaintance," I managed to release, quietly. "A friend from years ago."

Time slowed, and I swear my heart stopped beating. Numb. How I wanted to feel something more after hearing those dreadful words, that horrible sequence, that inevitable finish: Poland, round-up, Katyn, murdered with thousands of other Polish officers. I stopped listening. I shut down even before the major uttered the final word that summed up Emil's life. Gone.

"I'm sorry." That's all the major said.

I tried to make conversation, act as if I hadn't been dealt a blow, but he must have known, seen it before, the vacant look of a lost child without focus or direction. I was glad when the major closed the door behind him.

At the end, Albert had a summation, but there was no moral to Emil's life, no hook on which to hang my hopes. Emil had bad luck. Wrong place. That was my story, too. When the trigger caught the fold of my coat, the gangrene spread, and I forfeited my leg. I was disgusted by my misfortune, and that's how I imagined Emil would have felt about his. Though he died through no fault of his own, he would have been appalled by how his life ended in such an inadequate and arbitrary way. Before he could make his mark. It's the worst way to die.

In the coming days, I touched that worn shell that I'd kept in my purse all these years. Maybe that's why I couldn't get off the merry-go-round in my mind. Fragments of his vibrant life—his strong hands, the chords of his back, the scent of his body—would pop up in the small moments of the day. I kept telling myself it was pointless to dwell on Emil. Horrible, unnatural, untimely death was all around, and in that way, Emil's death was unremarkable. It's possible I was denial—an emotion unwittingly encouraged by de Guelis and the single word he used to describe Emil's status: Gone. It was as if my old lover had packed up and moved away unexpectedly—and now he was living in a new town. But there was no denying that I'd pushed Emil away for so long that now, with his passing, waves of remembrance kept returning him to me. I know that I'd never stopped caring. And now, fully healed, it was too late.

The anger and loneliness never left me. But I took some comfort in knowing I had survived many disappointments in my life: the loss of my leg and my dream of being a diplomat, the death of agents around me, and now Emil. But I had the strength that comes with being a survivor who had been given a second chance at a full life. And dammit, I wasn't going to waste it.

I had a job to do in Haute Loire, and I would stay to finish it.

CHAPTER EIGHT

The woman who limps is the most dangerous Allied agent in France.
We must find and destroy her.

Gestapo Wanted Poster

NOVEMBER 1941, LYON

Though only in place a few months, Heckler was receiving accolades on Baker Street for its secret reporting. I ignored their praise.

It isn't the spotlight that bothers me, and God knows I'm not shy. In school plays I always took the lead role, the pirate king. But praise and awards are a colossal waste of energy and a massive distraction, and if I averted my eyes and paid any attention at all to the superfluous musings of London, I'd slip up. I say, stay focused. Maintain discipline. Keep your edge sharp.

In being deaf to the praise, I wouldn't be mired in gratuitous reflection and admiration for my creation. I'd be free to think more clearly about what Heckler was and what it could become. As the organizer of Heckler, the first British network behind the lines in Vichy France, I was keenly aware of my power to shape my circuit. It was developing into a first-rate collector of intelligence, the eyes and ears Buck and Vera wanted, but that wasn't enough. Heckler was evolving, becoming something bigger, more important than merely a reporter of information. I desperately wanted my circuit to be of immense value to the larger war in France.

History was on my side; it had been my favorite subject at the *Ecole des Sciences Politiques* in Paris. Since the time of the Romans, Goths, and Gauls, the Haute Loire had been the crossroads of civilization. Crusaders walked the dusty Camino de Santiago—the way of Saint James—from the Holy Lands, through the region, to retake Spain. France's enemies understood. Seize Lyon, the region's largest city, and the rest would fall. History convinced me. My circuit was central to British success in retaking France.

I considered Heckler's strengths and determined that what our cause needed most was a stable platform in a hostile sea, a secure way station, a safe haven for agents and military trainers and pilots in desperate need. Heckler could offer safe houses and food, money and medical support. Our reporting would be the best around. It had to be. I'd push the boundaries by traveling to areas off limits to my British counterparts and issue reports they could not. For now, that's how Heckler could have the greatest impact.

There was so much to do, and all the pieces to the jigsaw puzzle were not fitting together. Most infuriating? My communications with London were painfully slow for my reports and maps. President Roosevelt's friend and emissary in Vichy, Ambassador Leahy, agreed that I should have access to the US Embassy's diplomatic pouch.

Still, I made few trips to the US embassy. The fewer US diplomats that knew my name or mission, the better and I was grateful the ambassador didn't ask questions, which was for the best. Using the pouch was a breach of diplomatic protocol and violated America's neutrality. But the more practical reason for using the pouch so sparingly was that it was so godawful slow. Good God. Pouched reports would travel overland and then by ship, then land again and go first to the American Embassy in London before being handed over to the Brits, who had their own byzantine routing system. My cables to my cutout, George Backer at the *Post* back in New York, weren't much faster. Nothing arrived on time. That was the way it was between Land-27—SOE's codename for France—and *chez nous*.

Those of us working in France in the fall of 1941 were at our wits' end. What I wanted, what SOE in France needed urgently, were more wireless sets and pianists. SOE had only one wireless operator; the Frenchman codenamed Noble in the OZ—the Occupied Zone, dropped blind at a time when there were no organized circuits to offer any support. Now, without more pianists, we were stymied. Lysander drops had to be arranged far in advance, new agents couldn't be vetted quickly by London CE, which was powerless to warn us quickly of gestapo traps. All of it kept British intelligence from growing its agent networks in France.

The only pianist in France, Noble, was working for Lucas's circuit, Autogiro, southwest of Paris. London promised that a second operator, George Nine, would arrive soon.

As Major de Guelis had said, Lucas was responsible for the reception of military trainers parachuting into the OZ, scheduled for October. The Corsicans would be the first wave of saboteurs, and all of us hoped desperately that this latest drop would include another pianist. When I received an urgent note in Doctor Rousset's letterbox requesting a meeting with Lucas, a man I'd never met, I had a suspicion that trouble might be at hand.

It was a gray, windy day in late November, and my breath hung still like a cloud in midair. Lucas was standing on the second bridge over the Saone, the Pont St. George, on the edge of old-town Lyon. He looked up from the river and after passing the appropriate passwords, we walked together swiftly over the horizon of the old stone structure and toward an empty traboule near the old Cathedral St. Jean.

*   *   *

Before my mission to France began, Vera took me aside and told me about the Frenchman codenamed Lucas. He seemed to have some inexplicable hold on her. I wanted to know more.

"His true name is Pierre de Vomecourt, and he comes from a long line of French aristocrats," she said. Vera wasn't easily affected, and never by title or good looks alone. Talent and courage captured Vera's attention.

"His family has only known tragedy. Generations of tragedy. It's what they call their glorious burden. Lucas's grandfather was tortured, then killed by the Germans in the *Guerre franco-allemande*, and his father, an army volunteer late in life, fought the Germans in the last war." Then in an off-handed, almost indifferent way, she added, "His father died in the Great War. The same grisly conflict that critically wounded Lucas's older brother, Jean."

"Lucas was evacuated from Dunkerque and parachuted back into the occupied zone six months ago. And now, his brothers jumped into the fight and are operating in France as well. Lucas is in the OZ; Gauthier to the south, the Unoccupied Zone; and Jean in the east along the Swiss border. There are so few of you in France. Your path will cross with the de Vomecourt brothers eventually. You'll see."

As Vera spoke, I pictured in my mind the kind of person Lucas might be. His family history probably had turned him into a hard, bitter man, maybe with a touch of aristocratic self-importance. But as Lucas extended his hand and locked his eyes onto my own, I sensed a mystical quality, a tranquility, a personal gravity—subtle like the moon that, without effort, could coax the sea back to shore. Vera had told me that only those who live closest to death truly know the meaning of life. Death had become so personal for Lucas. That could have been his secret.

Lucas had a narrow face, a high forehead that sloped back, and a mouth that revealed too many teeth when it broke into a laugh. But his lips drew tight once inside the traboule. He called me by the codename London had given him.

"You must remember, Germaine, that we were green. Frenchmen in England without a home, wishing only to be dropped into our country to fight. My brothers and I—and Noble of course—were the first bastard children. After Noble and I fled the rout at Dunkerque, we took commissions in the British army." He looked down the empty traboule toward the point of light that was its entrance. "But even now de Gaulle in London is focused on politics, so we are on our own. We arrived in Britain with nothing and departed for France with only a determination to liberate our country.

"We are an army of amateurs—bankers, lawyers, and merchants—with no knowledge of how to set up a resistance network. The British had no circuits. You are the first. You had training, you were given money. We were given a few francs and a radio and sent on our way. We were an experiment."

Lucas looked up at the arched stone ceiling. "Many mistakes were made. Many costly mistakes. Some come to France thinking it is a game we play. Cat and mouse with the Germans. But soon it becomes a deadly game. Last month, Autogiro arranged to bring the Corsicans to France. These men, all five, were saboteurs, the nucleus, to train resistance fighters to take back France. But the drop." Lucas's voiced lowered. "It did not go as planned.

"On the night of the full moon, as their parachutes fluttered to the ground, a traitor tipped off the Germans about the landing outside of Bergerac. Their supplies were captured, but the landing of men was off-course and the Corsicans scattered. They made their escape south to Marseilles.

"Again, I say, we are green. All were given the address of the safe house, the Villa des Bois, in Marseilles, and told to commit it to memory. But one, Tuberville, could not rely on his mind, so he wrote the address on a piece of paper and stuffed it in his pocket. When this agent was taken by the police, he was searched, and the Villa de Bois became known to the authorities. The Villa became a mousetrap.

"One by one, the Corsicans made their way to the Villa, and the gestapo was waiting to scoop them up. Within a month of their landing, all were prisoners. Even my compatriot, the pianist Noble, was lured into this Villa mouse trap."

Lucas looked at his feet and fell silent. "But the pain does not stop there. In the absence of Noble, my reliance on the new pianist, George Nine, grew and led him to spend much time on his wireless. He moved from place to place to avoid the gestapo's men. For a while, George Nine was able to evade the Germans. To reduce the time he spent on-air, he used Noble's technique. He told London to use the

BBC radio, personal messages in code, to confirm air drops. But the gestapo's men soon located the transmitter. They found George Nine. He was shot in the back of his head."

Lucas looked down, seeming to consider the blow. His broad forehead furrowed, and his voice turned so low I could barely hear his next words. "Now, I am without my partner and friend. But this pain is not for me alone. We all suffer losses. But perhaps not one so great. All of us who report to London are without a wireless. So my only avenue to SOE is by courier through Heckler. You must report this information back to London and tell them of the Corsican's capture and our need for more pianists."

"Of course," I said, "but how will you continue?"

"I have an idea. But first, let me speak of a confession. I am an impatient man. That is my weakness. One of many. The French circuit Gloria relies on me to transmit secrets from its spies watching the German navy. But now I cannot help them. I cannot wait for a new wireless operator to arrive, so I have made contact with the Polish circuit, Interallied, in Paris. The woman they call Le Chatte has a wireless I can use on SOE frequencies, but I need you to report all of this through your channels to London. Until then, I will use a priest to courier information to you."

Did I hear him right? Alesh? Before I could ask, Lucas pushed on.

"I know I am asking much. But I have another very special request. There are so few of us in France, but I know that you have contacts in the south. You offer my only hope. You must free these men from jail in Marseilles."

My jaw slackened, and I stayed silent for what seemed like hours. Had I heard Lucas correctly? Pass information, yes, certainly; I'd done that before. But arrange a jailbreak from Marseilles, hundreds of miles from Lyon? My mind was racing. Lucas was a man in need. Desperate need. He wouldn't have asked unless he had run out of options.

Christine 25—the agent I had moved to Marseilles was now working with the Urchin circuit. Perhaps she could help. I had to try.

"I'll make the arrangements," I said.

"Good. This will not be easy. The Corsicans are charged with a capital offense, crimes against the state. The penalty is great. Death. So you must work quickly."

The jailbreak was the second half of Lucas's request. Heckler would be a pass-through for Autogiro's reports to London. But the courier. The priest. It could only be Alesh. He'd be returning to Lyon.

"This courier," I said. "Tell me, is it the abbe, Alesh? I have grown suspicious of him," I said, not waiting for a response. "Do you trust him?"

"I had not thought of Alesh, the priest, a traitor. He came to me through Armand in the Interallied network. They trust him, and the priest is known to many as a strong supporter of de Gaulle. But these days, everyone must prove themselves beyond suspicion, and he has not yet aroused mine. I will pay close attention to the abbe's movements. But for now, I have no choice. I must use the priest who can slip so easily between the lines."

*   *   *

I sent an urgent note to Christine 25 and two days later met her at the train station in Marseilles. It could only be a quick meeting, too dangerous to linger under the watchful eyes of the gestapo patrolling the station. We stood side by side on the platform without glancing at each other.

"Our friends, the Corsicans, are no longer here," Christine said, looking over her shoulder. "They are in Perigueux—Beleyme Prison—one of the worst shitholes in all of France. Overrun by vermin and filth . . ." She handed me a *La Tribune,* the newspaper of Le Puy. "Check the classifieds. I've made an appointment for you. I have a friend who might help." She turned her back and walked away.

I placed the folded newspaper in my handbag, walked forward to cross the tracks, and stepped onto the next platform for the 3:15 back to Lyon.

The top of the paper was poking out from my bag, and there it would stay until I was safely onboard. That day, good tradecraft paid off. As the sliding door to my compartment opened, I was met by a cloud of cigarette smoke. Three German soldiers, startled, stared up at me in unison.

I had made it a rule never to avoid Germans, so I voluntarily sat with them in their compartment. It presented an opportunity. I would stay silent and sometimes engage them in their native tongue. It was surprising what I learned: where they were moving next, their complaints about their wives and their leaders, the results of their children's soccer games and of British bombs. When listening, I acted detached but made mental notes of what they said and what they didn't and maneuvered the conversation when I could. The way they held themselves and positioned their bodies told me more about their morale than by what they said. I strained the information, all of it, and the best nuggets went back to London.

These men weren't gestapo, thank God, just enlisted, and though I limped into the compartment, they didn't seem interested in Cuthbert. My wooden companion was still beneath my long woolen dress. Word of the limping lady might not have filtered down.

I opened *Gone with the Wind* and continued to listen. The soldier to my right with a nasty scar across his face, offered a Gitanes. I couldn't refuse a regulated pleasure. The one directly across from me, a pudgy corporal who overflowed his belt, drifted in and out of sleep, then woke with a snort. Embarrassed, he immediately asked to look at my newspaper. I handed it over without a second thought. He glanced at the banner, sniffed, and then returned it.

"Yes," I said, "it's true, Le Puy isn't Paris. The local news isn't all that interesting." I placed it back in my handbag. As much as I detest Germans, I can be congenial, because the unpleasant are suspect. Still, I was relieved when the three got off at the next stop. Two Frenchmen entered my compartment. I opened my *La Tribune*.

I didn't reach the classifieds immediately. I started in a deliberate manner from front to back. Nothing to arouse suspicion or curiosity. At the page of interest, Christine 25 had circled the name of Monsieur Pebellier, the mayor of Le Puy. Four numbers had been scribbled at the bottom of the page: 25-11-16-15. A Vichy mayor as an intelligence source? I smiled. *Bien joué*, Christine. Today was November 24, 1941. I would meet Pebellier the next day at 4:15 PM.

I was ushered into the mayor's office, and after the thick oak door clicked shut, I introduced myself as Virginia Hall of the *Post*, and Suzanne Bertillon's supervisor. Not wanting to arouse suspicion, I couldn't trust Pebellier, I remained vague about my visit.

The mayor, a bald man who appeared wider than tall, was dressed in a gray threadbare suit. A small black bowtie lay mostly buried under a huge flap of skin that wagged as he spoke.

"I grew up in Suzanne Bertillon's hometown, you know. Montpellier." Pebellier said. "I worked for a time with her father in the mill. That is where I met Suzanne. When she was young."

"Monsieur," I said, "I have little time to play games. The Suzanne I employ grew up on Avenue Marceau in Paris, and her father died when she was young. So let's speak of real people, shall we?"

Pebellier stood and started pacing.

"You must understand, Miss Hall," the mayor said, considering his words. "For a time, I was in jail without knowing if I would return to Le Puy alive. Yes, it is unusual that someone with my background would be elected mayor. But I am in this position because I know people and can help many, and that precisely is why you are here, is it not? I am a man still under suspicion. The gestapo has a long memory, so I must remain careful."

Christine, maintaining security, probably had not offered the mayor much about the Corsicans. As my eyes followed the mayor pacing the room, I spoke in elliptical terms of my dilemma. Then I said that five friends were in Beleyme prison.

The mayor stopped mid-step and looked at me. His face tightened, and his eyes grew small. "Sometimes it is more fortunate to be killed resisting arrest. The prison, Beleyme in Perigueux. You do know it is the worst of all prisons. Living in excrement. And the food . . . starvation is preferable to the disease the daily meal brings. They are in peril merely by being held in such a place."

I nodded in agreement. "I must get them out. And quickly. I have been thinking. What if I were to make a financial contribution to a prison guard or warden?"

"Hmmm . . . yes, we seek the goal of release, but your approach lacks an understanding of the subtleties of French justice and the requirements for freedom. Some prison guards are French subjects and Petain loyalists, but they also have much to lose. If they are caught, well, there is no one so despised in Beleyme as a prison guard who is now himself a prisoner."

Pebellier bowed his head and massaged the skin beneath his chin. "Let me think."

After a few moments, the mayor turned his head up toward the ceiling. "Yes. I suppose we should consider this a drama of three acts. First, we must obstruct the prosecution's case, while we work to have the five remanded to another—how shall we say—more *lenient* milieu. Perhaps a prison close to Le Puy, where we have control over the environment. And then, finally, quietly and without agitation, we will have them slip from sight."

He turned his face toward me. "French lawyers," Pebellier said with slight smile, "specialize in the art of obstruction." The mayor then swept his index finger through the air. "At this, no lawyer in the world can compare. But . . . like magic we'll need to make evidence disappear. Once this happens, then, well, the lawyers can throw their hands up into the air and claim an outrage. What kind of legal system would permit such a trial without evidence? Why would Vichy allow this mockery of justice to take place?"

The mayor then returned to his seat, and his voice calmed. "But, of course, this is France, and I cannot guarantee any outcome. That is why we must plan to move the prisoners. I can find lawyers who for a fee will try to derail a trial, but assigning five men to another prison, well, this is beyond my abilities. For that, you will need powerful allies."

*   *   *

As I prepared for bed at the Grand Nouvelle, Cuthbert seemed particularly ornery. I must have wrenched my knee leaving the mayor's office, landing awkwardly. My wooden companion was angry about his treatment, and I admit in the past weeks to paying him little heed.

I began removing the straps around my waist. I had the outline of a plan, but not much more. Bribing lawyers to slow the trial was only the first step. Having the Corsicans moved to a local prison, then out of the jail, then to a safe house, then out of the country—all away from the searching eyes of the gestapo? The mayor was wrong. This was more than a three-act play, and each presenting its own set of dangerous obstacles.

Cuthbert and his straps were off and my stump sock was wet where blisters had formed then burst. The scar across my stump was red and enflamed. I'd experienced some discomfort recently, but I had thought it was no more than usual. Maybe it was something a bit more than discomfort. But with all the activity swirling around, well, I had a job to do. Cuthbert. Sure, he was angry, but dammit, I was too. I swore at him. Told him to shape up and stop being a pain in the ass. Then I cooled a bit and cleaned my stump. A fleeting thought: I should lay off Cuthbert for a day. But the idea passed quickly. So many were depending on me.

*   *   *

The next day, I made a quick trip to the Town Hall and handed the mayor an envelope containing 20,000 francs and a note telling him to contact me through the letter box in Doctor Rousset's office if he needed more assistance. This would be our last face-to-face meeting. It was time to move into the shadows and distance myself from the mayor.

It's strange how sometimes you set your mind on a problem and without thinking about it directly, you come up with the seed of an idea. My most immediate concern was finding the powerful ally. It occurred to me that Ambassador Leahy had the gravitas to bring attention to any issue and, best of all, the ambassador was sympathetic to the British cause.

When I met with the ambassador, I spoke elliptically, of course, about myself but recommended that the embassy intervene for humanitarian reasons on behalf of the men.

Ambassador Leahy said he would not circumvent French justice by seeking a pardon—no, he would seek an *accommodation* in moving them out of the wretched conditions of Belemye prison. Something might be done to move the prisoners closer to family members. Perhaps to Mauzac Prison on the Dordogne.

As I got up to leave, the ambassador reached out to grab my hand. He asked me to work through his military attaché, Captain Scou. "He's a man of great ability," Ambassador Leahy said. "Someone you can trust."

CHAPTER NINE

—————

*My father loved the country and spent a lot of time with his children
teaching them about the flora and fauna of the countryside of
Maryland. He was a most capable person in every respect—
friendly, well-liked, extraordinarily well-respected,
and quite well-travelled.*

VIRGINIA HALL

Everyone has a special talent. Father's gift? He could make anyone laugh, and maybe he was loved so because he didn't judge anyone. Even as the Depression laid many low, Father's silly jokes made even the most defeated stranger crack a smile.

He was an entrepreneur—real estate—and he launched several movie houses, too. Movies were a good fit for Father's good-natured personality. These weren't grand palaces with gilded spires and huge auditoriums. No, he built a few neighborhood nickel-and-dime cinemas, where the regular folk could go to forget their worries. John and I took tickets and ran the concession, and Mother, well-groomed in a stylish black and silver feathered headpiece, was Father's secretary.

Some thought Mother was the brains of the business, but in truth, my parents were evenly matched. Father brought the people in, and mother understood finances and kept the enterprise afloat. Though upright and reserved, Mother was never starchy or preachy. You could call her principled, I suppose, and she wasn't one to stay clean when there was work to be done. They were a good team, Mother and Father, and they were devoted to each other.

I saw every film my father brought to town. The adventure movies more than once. Mother would say I was too dramatic as a child, but Father, feigning some disappointment, would roll down his evening newspaper and say, "Oh, Barbara, let Dindy be."

I had an imagination that couldn't be tamed. I'd lay awake at night and fancy myself as Mary Pickford in *Pollyanna*—a pixie with a penchant for getting into trouble. Dreaming, dreaming, picturing life as someone else, trying on different roles. When I was older, I channeled my fantasies into productions at Roland Park School for Girls. I wasn't shy. In one school play, *A Thousand Years Ago*, I was an old man in heavy clothes and a beard. I enjoyed every minute of that role, hiding behind the words and appearance of someone I'd created. The feeling of not being known or discovered was addictive, like a narcotic. I found a special kind of freedom in being hidden.

And in my mind, while I was Mary Pickford, my dear father was Douglas Fairbanks junior in *The Black Pirate*, riding down a ship's sail on the point of a knife. That image of the Halls with a swashbuckling past had a morsel of truth.

Early in the evening before going up to bed, my father would sit in his big overstuffed chair, his head buried in the paper, wearing his favorite striped sweater that held the faint scent of pipe tobacco. I'd climb under his paper and into his welcoming arms and ask him to tell again the story of how Grandfather Hall at age nine had stowed away in the belly of a schooner bound for Baltimore. He'd finish by saying the Halls were a family of risk takers. The willingness to risk it all seemed to have passed its way through the generations from Grandfather to Father and beyond.

Our family lived in a series of rented brownstone apartments with white marble steps in Baltimore until Father could afford to build his theater business. It was only later that he purchased Box Horn, our first and only real home, and even then, he didn't tell Mother when he bought it. Not that she minded. She loved life on the farm, having grown up on one herself; owning theaters and the farm in the middle of the Depression was a gamble that paid off. It seems the Halls were one of the families in the neighborhood with food on the table.

But there were lean times, too. Father lost money in the crash. To augment what the theaters brought in and the food from the farm, we, like a lot of folks, had a large garden and hunted the back woods. All the Halls could handle a gun, including Mother. She was a good shot—as good a shot as any man in town. And that streak of justice in her, well, it revealed itself in the hunt and extended to all living things, man or beast.

When I was old enough to lift a rifle, I was only allowed to shoot at tin cans and wooden targets for practice. Mother said whenever I raised my gun to shoot something alive, I better have a good reason. If I raised my gun, well then, she expected me to pull the trigger—said she wanted me to think about the why as well as what was in my sight, so when the time came, there would be no hesitation and my shot would be straight and clean and true. It was a difficult lesson to learn. I hunted deer, pheasant, and other game and could gut and clean them, too. But early on, I tested my skills against varmints.

One day just as the sun was setting, I shot a big old possum walking across a log, and somehow my mother heard about it. Maybe John snitched on me.

She told me, "I want you to go fetch that possum and bring him home." Her voice was stern and unyielding, so I had to obey. I carried it by the tail, and when I dropped it on the front porch, mother said, "Okay, now you skin it and clean it. You're going to eat that possum you killed. You might think that's a worthless animal. But the Halls don't kill for no reason."

I was angry, mostly at John for tattling on me, and I was headstrong, too, but I obeyed. Mother had a pot of water boiling away on the stove, just waiting for me.

Then she told me a story about when she was growing up. Times were tough, and sometimes possum and squirrel were all that was around to eat. "Animals are here for a purpose," she said.

She showed me how to cook the possum, and that night, while Father and John ate chicken, Mother and I ate possum.

At first, I hated her for making me eat that old varmint. Especially in front of John. It was gamey and greasy, sour like a catfish wallowing in the mudflats, and it had parts I had never seen before. But in some strange way, as much as I hated her for making me eat that long-tailed rodent, well, that lesson brought us closer.

The years passed, and I left for the State Department. Then came the shock of Father's sudden death, a stroke early in life. John lost his job at the brick factory and left the farm to look for work. Mother was a strong woman, but now she was on her own in that big old house. All alone on the farm.

But without anyone supporting Mother, she still was supporting me. She was the only person I ever told that I was a spy for British intelligence. At her insistence, SOE gave her a post office box number to send me letters. Through the years and my different assignments, she wrote regularly. Eventually, I received those letters, but only after I returned from the field.

DECEMBER 1941, VICHY

My God. It was the last thing you'd expect: death on a peaceful Sunday morning. Torpedoes and bombs broke the stillness. Explosions, black clouds billowing, seamen struggling through oily water and flames, and those boys, all those young boys, trapped, straining to breathe in that sinking ship. I almost couldn't say the words. Pearl Harbor.

News usually came late in my part of the world, and it when it did arrive, the truth was boiled and strained through the censors' filter. It towed the Vichy line. And if it came from halfway around the globe? Sometimes it never made it here.

But Pearl Harbor was different. The evening of December seventh, I'd just finished dinner in the hotel restaurant—cabbage stuffed with stale bread and chestnuts—and I was sipping a cup of coffee, sour, like it was brewed through my stump sock, when it occurred to me, the next day was December eighth. Had it been eight years since Gediz?

I don't dwell on the past but that's an anniversary I can't forget, and that evening I was lost in a daydream about Cuthbert, and how we were making our way in the world. Then the porter came in, called my name, and handed me the telegram that pulled me rudely into the present. It startled me. Most of my urgent messages are in code and come through the embassy or by letterbox.

But this telegram was in clear text and didn't come from SOE London. No, I received the first word from George Backer, my cutout at the *Post*. The telegram was marked urgent, and Backer wrote in a terse and breathless way, not to tell me about the breaking news so much as to demand I actually report on it. Seems his bosses in New York sent out an urgent plea to all their stringers covering the globe to get the public's reaction. Of all things, they wanted to put me to work.

Like all Americans, I was stunned by the events in Hawaii. Surprise and shock were my first responses. But my next thought after hearing of that unspeakable treachery? Being an American, I was ashamed to admit it, but it was undeniable. I felt relief. As terrible and as tragic as the attack was, it finally got America off its ass and into this goddam war. God knows we needed the Americans' help.

Preparing for bed that evening, it occurred to me how little it had taken to convince me to join the fight that America had not yet entered. Buck and Vera had offered an adventure, and I had taken it. Maybe I had a chip on my shoulder, something to prove to all the naysayers: that Cuthbert and I, if given a second chance, could make something of our lives together. But over time, my bravado had softened and my reasons for staying had deepened.

It might have been too sentimental to say, I'm not that way, but once here, I was moved by the quiet, desperate lives of ordinary Frenchman and the plight of the Jews. How they'd been bullied by the Germans and lost everything—their homes, their worldly possessions, and most important, their freedom and lives.

As the Nazis' gruesome plans came to light, my anger grew. They'd destroy everything that wasn't physically perfect or ethnically pure. In the quiet of the night, I returned to Gediz and my wound, and Cuthbert, and I knew I couldn't live—or be allowed to live—in a hate-filled world ruled by someone's twisted view of perfection. Emil's death and the bombs falling on Oahu had given me more reasons to stay. Then I thought of our country, Maryland, Box Horn Farm, my brother John, and father Ned, and Barbara, my mother, and others like me, who'd suffered wounds and weren't considered "good enough." And here I was in France. On the front. Fighting for all of them.

* * *

I expected London to reach out to say how America's entry would change my life in this corner of the world, so I checked my *boite aux lettres* in the US Embassy regularly. Walking past the guards and through the huge front doors, I was struck by the frenetic pace—people scurrying about busily, cardboard boxes stacked high, and polished furniture lining the halls like soldiers on parade. The embassy was being reduced. "Essential personnel only," they said, and the upright Marine guarding the code room door whispered that if I were smart, I'd be leaving, too.

Communications from London still were painfully slow, and I was sure my bosses in the Special Operations Executive were studying how America's entry into the war would affect all of us overseas.

Days later, I found a sealed envelope and a coded message waiting for me. It was short:

```
PM said 7 December best day of terrible war.
Your American documents now a liability.
MI-6 says a Paris circuit penetrated.  No
specifics. More pianists coming. Vera
```

I tore the message and tossed the remnants into the embassy burn bag.

Vera, my mentor and Buck's second back at SOE, didn't need to tell me that my life now was in greater jeopardy. I was the enemy. My cover as a journalist for the *New York Evening Post*? Of little use. With America in the war, all of us in unoccupied France were suspected spies. The US Embassy recommended that Americans pack up and go home. Those who remained, even embassy staff officers with a legitimate reason to stay, were followed by the secret police. Tailed, questioned, detained, deported.

But the greatest penalties were reserved for Americans crossing into the German Occupied Zone. Just being in the OZ would land you in a labor camp. If you were lucky, you'd be interned in Drancy outside Paris for the rest of the war, but if you were caught spying on the German side of the line? There'd be a special room waiting for you. No one would hear your screams or see you carted off to Buchenwald, Ravensbruck, or some other godforsaken death camp.

I fought the panic and weariness that came with thinking day-af-ter-day that all eyes were on me. Tightening my espionage tradecraft helped me cope. It gave me the confidence to know when I was free of tails and could conduct agent meetings in that now more dangerous environment.

To combat any lingering paranoia, I pushed my identity deeper into the shadows. I moved from Lyon and took up residence at the Hotel de la Paix in Vichy just down from gestapo headquarters. The hotel was like many others, an acceptable, unassuming plain-faced building with black shutters and a small lobby. Quaint. But by far, the hotel's most endearing quality was its proprietor, a gaunt old gent with a toothless grin. The dear man never asked me to sign the hotel register.

But it wasn't enough just to change my address. I filed one more *Post* article, and then Virginia Hall, American journalist, quietly vanished to be replaced by a French woman with a *carte d'identitè* that bore the name Brigitte LeContre.

Brigitte LeContre slid easily off my tongue. This alias, was it too bold, too showy, too memorable for my enemies? Brigitte LeContre. Did it reflect a touch of narcissism? I lingered on the thought, uneasy that I might in some small way, and without awareness, change my personality if only to reflect my new stylish name. If imprudent, I'd change it, but for now I'd mask any superficial haughtiness by clothing her, like all my characters, as a frumpy commonplace figure who wouldn't raise the eyebrow of any man.

*   *   *

With my new identity, makeover, and accommodations, I could to turn my attention to the most troubling aspect of London's message: the penetration of the Paris circuit. London didn't say which one had been compromised—there were several in the German Occupied Zone—but chances were that Lucas, that impatient French nobleman without a wireless operator, was in the thick of it. Had he met the woman, Le Chatte, from that Polish circuit, Interallied, in Paris? Was it Interallied that had been burned? Lucas might be hiding. I had to find him if for no other reason than to warn him, learn what he knew, and report back to London. Surely his brother, Gauthier, would know where Lucas was.

I'd met Gauthier once before on his way to Marseilles. He needed no introduction that afternoon in the lobby of the Grand Nouvelle. His family breeding was all over his face—the same de Vomecourt forehead sloping back clean and open, his chestnut hair and horn-rimmed glasses, all of it unmistakably like his brother. And then there was the way he strode into the lobby. With supreme confidence.

That time in Lyon, Gauthier had been just passing through, looking for overnight accommodations, but I had suspected the real reason for his visit was that he was broke. Might I be willing to part with some spare francs? Of course, I had given him what I had—50,000 for his circuit, Ventriloquist, in the Unoccupied Zone, and an apartment for the night in the old quarter of Lyon. If I'd had more, I'd have given it to him. There were so few of us.

I'd planned to see him again the next morning for breakfast, but Gauthier had vanished like a cool breeze on a hot day. Gone on the first train to Paris. It had been so easy for him to disappear, working for the French railroads as an inspector and carrying documents, legitimate documents, allowing him to travel freely about the country.

Now I needed Gauthier to reach his brother and warn him if it wasn't too late. But without a wireless, I could only spread the word among my agents and hope he'd be found. Gauthier could be anywhere traveling the rails.

MARCH 1942, VICHY

With America now in the fight, all of us were optimistic that the spigot finally would be opened and we'd soon be receiving the men and supplies we needed by Lizzy and trawler. We were wrong. The SOE agents that arrived came slowly, painfully so, in groups of four and five by air and sea, spread far apart. Still, all of them, as few as they were, seemed to be converging on my small circuit at one time, passing through, seeking money, board, and shelter.

Airmen shot down received medical attention from Doctor Rousset and refuge in safe houses offered by Madame Guerin before being sent to Spanish *passeurs* who guided the men for their arduous journey to freedom across the Pyrenees. One pilot, Watlington, was the first downed airman to visit. I called him my carrier pigeon because I had him bring coded reports back to London, as I would others. Major de Guelis had been right, Heckler was becoming as busy as Grand Central Station.

The two de Guelis said would join me, Olive and Alain, arrived by trawler and made their way to the Haute Loire, fortunately free of gestapo tails. Olive, a man with narrow lips and dark, drooping eyebrows, stayed long enough to help find pockets of resistance near Lyon before moving south to Marseilles to lead Urchin.

Alain, the sabotage instructor with jet black hair, a roguish smile, and an eye for the local women, had a more difficult time mustering support among the French, and really, it was too early to do anything but count heads. London hadn't given the green light for sabotage operations, and only a few Lizzies were dropping plastic explosives and weapons for stockpiling. So Alain, frustrated, did his best to set up his own small circuit not far from Lyon, but never did make a go of it.

The circuits were growing, but for every three steps forward, we took two steps back. During spring 1942, it seemed every British agent setting foot near Paris was being rolled up. Ten of fourteen met the fate of the Corsicans: arrested, detained, tortured, or killed by the secret police and gestapo, and by March, London believed

Lucas's Autogiro was the only British SOE circuit operating in the German Occupied Zone. Having seen neither hide nor hair of the de Vomecourt brothers, I had my doubts that any British circuit in the OZ was active.

Just as I was about to give up hope of seeing Gauthier again, he arrived at my doorstep. He told me straight off that he didn't know where his brother Lucas was, and without him, Autogiro was in disarray. All its officers were in hiding.

"I knew something would go terribly wrong," Gauthier said, "when I went to Interallied's safe house on Rue du Colonel Moll outside of Paris before Autogiro had collapsed. I'd heard its leader, Armand, was disorganized and had no common sense, but I saw it for myself. Detailed maps of agent locations were on the walls, copies of wireless cables were strewn about the floor, piles of intelligence reports sat on the desk. People walked in and out unchecked. There was no security. Interallied was a disaster.

"I told my brother, 'You are throwing your lot with Armand?' Lucas just shrugged and said, 'I have no choice. I support other networks, like the French circuit Gloria, and without a pianist of my own, I am a desperate man.' So he took a chance. He said Le Chatte would help him contact London."

"Now I am told Armand's agents of Interallied—postmen, railway workers, and yes, members of the gendarmerie—all are burned. Over one-hundred arrested. They are filling up the gaol in Fresnes and LaSante, awaiting interrogation. And my brother's fate is unknown. I can have no other conclusion than this Le Chatte is a double agent responsible for the destruction of Interallied and Autogiro. And yet I am told Interallied's radio still transmits."

APRIL 1942, LYON

The nurse was waiting for me at Dr. Rousset's clinic and quickly ushered me into the back room, which was barely large enough for an examination table and two chairs.

The Doctor entered a moment later, excited. "Marie, I have done as you instructed. A building outside of town is being renovated with room for beds and a kitchen. Of course, it will not be fully furnished as a clinic might be, but for your purposes, this is not needed."

The doctor had done well with 20,000 francs. "It is an old building," he said, "and will take time to complete. When must it be ready?"

"As quickly as you can."

"How many nurses do we need?"

"Just one with the utmost discretion," I said. "In a white uniform to make this building look the part. We'll need a small sign out front so no one will question the building's purpose. We don't want prying eyes."

The doctor smiled. "To create a clinic whose very purpose is to hide rather than help? There is something very unusual about this task you have given me." He looked down in thought. "Perhaps we should create a clinic for patients with a dread disease. Something that can be caught by others and is difficult to cure. Consumption. That should keep townspeople and the gestapo away."

"Yes, but when the authorities come, they'll want to speak with the patients, and our guests may not speak French."

"Ahhh . . . yes," the doctor said. "In that case, it must be an asylum. Yes, for the *malad* of mind. The Germans and secret police have no time or patience with those who exhibit such an illness. I will make a small sign saying this is an asylum for the insane.

"But now, you must sit," he said, pointing to the examination table. What he said next stunned me because of its candor. "Marie, you must remove your prosthesis, so I can examine your wound. On this I will not accept an objection."

I was too startled to protest. It wasn't the thought of removing Cuthbert for the doctor but that I'd been revealed so completely. Most disturbing.

"You hide your limp well," he said, "but recently I've seen a change in your walk and the expression on your face. I cannot have my favorite patient in discomfort, can I?"

In truth, Cuthbert had been trying my patience for the past month, but I hadn't known others could tell. With some reluctance, I began to remove his straps.

"I have other patients with amputations of the leg, though they older," the doctor said with a faint smile. "And some wounds come with delusions, the poison gas of the last Great War."

"I can assure you," I said, unbuckling the harness from my waist, "there was no glory in this wound. It was due to my own stupidity."

The doctor's face stiffened after my stump sock came off. It hurt when he touched the edges of my wound, gently, as he would an over-ripe melon. My stump had been oozing, and its sock, changed regularly, was wet with pus.

"Marie," he said, "there are signs of infection. I can clean your stump and give you some ointments, but unless you stay off your leg, the wound will become worse, as will your limp."

I nodded but didn't respond to the doctor's recommendation. The asylum had to be ready.

It seemed that Mayor Pebellier's lawyers had been successful in paying lawyers or displacing evidence. The Corsicans' trial had been delayed long enough for the Ambassador and Captain Scou to intervene. The three-part drama was entering a new phase. The Corsicans soon would be moving from Beyelme to Mauzac Military Prison north of Toulouse.

.

CHAPTER TEN

———

I don't wear my heart on my sleeve and have been brought up not to display undue emotion. I don't "talk it out" but have no problem expressing my opinions. Am I tactless, candid, and unsympathetic to others' feelings? I don't know. I can't say.

VIRGINIA HALL

Before leaving England, I had been ushered into a small room on Baker Street and handed a stack of papers to sign. My new paycheck was a good one, about two hundred dollars a month, and what few expenses I had in the field were covered by SOE. God knows anything left in France worth buying already had been stolen by the Germans, so I had my pay sent to my mother. Running the farm by herself, she needed it more than I.

I'd just finished poring through the stack—insurance, updating my will, the usual documents one signs before accepting hazardous duty—and had been preparing to leave when in walked a gruff old quartermaster, a square block of a man. One more paper, a single page, slid across the varnished surface. But it wasn't just any document, it was the State Secrets Act, ordering me to keep silent about my work overseas. The quartermaster wasn't through with me.

Standing, he'd splayed his stubby fingers on the table and leaned forward, his face inches from my own. He breathed in deeply, and when he exhaled, well, it was putrid like old milk that had spoiled in the afternoon sun. Lunch was stuck between his two big teeth; his white and red eyes, round and bulbous, were unblinking; his nostrils gaped like black caverns. He didn't say a word. He just stared at me. It seemed like a half hour.

Then he spoke. "I only have one question for you, missy. CAN YOU LIE, HALL? CAN YOU LIE?"

I'd thought his display more amusing than frightening. It was a reasonable question, though a bit dramatic, but lying isn't just a man's domain. I was one of Vera's best and didn't flinch, saying sweetly, "Yes, I can lie and do it well."

That's how my career in espionage had begun, by defending my ability to deceive. Since then, I'd admitted that spying was a difficult life—living alone behind the walls of a safe house under an assumed name, working a fictitious job, communicating through cutouts and letterboxes. Meeting people only when it couldn't be done any other way. I didn't reveal myself even to fellow agents, because they could have given me up as easily through an unguarded comment as they would under gestapo torture.

I became a blank slate. I stayed quiet and listened. I gathered what others said without saying much of anything myself. But these past months when my agents, my friends, and my lover had been captured and killed, well, I suppose it was natural to pull back behind my fortress walls. For my own protection.

But agents must fight the temptation to withdraw. We made easy targets standing still, and our self-imposed exile would save no one.

I'd learned over these past months that the German mind was formidable: ruthless, precise, focused. Military Intelligence gathered the smallest scraps of information and then, as if arranging bits of tile in a mosaic, it worked relentlessly to put the pieces together. Soon the composite picture would emerge of who you really were, and your rampart would start to crumble stone by stone. More bits of information, more stones would fall until there was nothing to protect you, and you were left standing there, a naked spy.

Once captured, the cruelty would begin. You'd be horrified by how calmly your interrogator spoke of unspeakable things. You'd turn blue, he would say, and suffocate in a tub of ice water. You'd stiffen as a hot electric current passed through your body. You'd writhe on the floor after acid was injected into your veins. He would tell you without emotion, then watch the terror cross your face. It was his job: dispensing pain. Inflicting suffering.

You'd try reason with him. Offer something. Just a little bit. He would smile, knowing your door had opened. You both knew there was more and he wouldn't be satisfied. Ever. He could give you a slow painful death, and he wanted it all: locations, activities, people. You'd try to hold out. You'd try to be brave. Then it would start again, and you'd talk again to stop the pain. And you both knew it. You'd give up your fellow agents and they would be hunted and questioned. And the circle would expand diabolically, inexorably, until no one was left.

Audacity was the only way to defeat the German mind. They didn't expect their enemy to live among them. Why did airman shot down over enemy territory hide in brothels used exclusively by the Germans? They were never searched. Who would the Germans find but other Germans? So you would engage the Nazis where they lived and worked. You'd exploit their chauvinism, flirt and laugh, use the best weapon you had, the same one they would deny you: your humanity.

You held the enemy close and lived by deception. You sharpened your wits and your skill to manipulate. You did it so often it became second nature. It became enmeshed in your personality. It was part of who you were, and it didn't bother you, because you were absolutely convinced it was the only way to stay alive.

Take Guerin. There was a connection—friendship was too strong a word; it was something more like fondness. I told her couple things about myself, toss-aways, which I gave freely. But after Emil's death, something took hold of me—maybe it was a seriousness, a greater focus—and I began to understand the bigger issues of war and the need to win at all cost. Now there was a price to my friendship, if you could call it that. I would only reveal a small piece of myself if there was something larger to gain. Nothing was for free.

Months ago, I'd told Madame Guerin about Emil's death,

knowing it would strengthen the connection and help me get more support. Was that manipulation? Of course. Did I feel guilty? No. No guilt. No remorse. Nothing of the kind. Early in my life, I might have regretted acting that way, but now it felt natural. It felt organic. And when I got what I wanted? Dare I say? It felt good.

Would Guerin have been so willing to assist had I not told her about my beau's untimely death? Perhaps. But I had tugged on her heartstrings and given her another reason to help. She had two more safe houses to offer.

"Might you provide board and clothing, too?" I asked, softly. Guerin quickly said yes, and that wasn't the end of her giving.

LATE APRIL 1942, LYON

We were in the courtyard behind Madame Guerin's *Maison.* The midmorning sun had begun to break up the cold mist, still low on the ground.

"You know, Marie," Guerin said, pushing a stream of Gauloise into the fresh air, "the girls say more German soldiers are moving to the front now that the Americans are in the war. The bastards are starting to use the Vichy gendarme to guard the prisons and the border."

I offered a silent nod. Good news. I'd just received word from Captain Scou that the five Corsicans were in Mauzac Military prison on the banks of the Dordogne. An escape might be easier if the guards were local Vichy police. As for getting the prisoners moved from the wretched Beyelme prison? It seemed the good Ambassador also was a good politician. He had leverage and used it. America was silently providing food to the starving in Vichy France.

*   *   *

"London says you're to contact Madame Bloch in Villamblard," Gregoire, my new pianist said, as he removed his headphones and pulled its cord from his wireless set. SOE had kept its pledge by dropping several pianists that spring—still not nearly enough—and I kept mine at arm's length. Not that I distrusted Gregoire, but the gestapo had begun an aggressive hunt for pianists using new direction-finding airplanes, and it wasn't safe for us to be together. It was merely by chance that I was there that morning, but it pleased me no end to get the news first hand. The wait was over. The curtain was rising on the last act for the Corsicans.

Madame Bloch, wife of the group's leader, Jean-Pierre, was witting of my role in planning and executing the prison break, and I traveled to her home to learn more about the prison and its security and to finalize details for the escape.

Gaby Bloch, a petite brunette with narrow features, had a baguette peeking from a brown bag under her arm as I arrived at her modest fieldstone house with terracotta roof. She was rushing out the door and had a wild, distracted look.

"Beyelme for Mauzac, we thought it a good exchange," she said in a low tone. "But there's no food, and Jean-Pierre's prison uniform falls straight around him as if it were still on a hanger. And his face, so gray, so thin." She paused and looked up at a heavy cloud drifting overhead and then down the muddy road.

"My children haven't seen their father for many months, and they call out, but his voice is silent. I show them pictures so they won't forget. Be patient, I say, your father will come home." Gaby, lost in the moment, gazed at a bicycle leaning against a nearby maple. "I cannot talk now," she said. "I will return from Mauzac this evening. You may stay the night."

I made good use of my day in the dense deciduous hills above the prison. The oaks and maples had leafed out light emerald, and I found a comfortable old log resting in moss midway up a hill. The compound was fully in view, but the surrounding brush hid me from below. Slowly, as I began to unbuckle my harness, Dr. Rousset's words about Cuthbert came to mind. How he needed more care. More soothing. Rest.

"What am I going to do with you?" I said softly. "I violated our truce. Pushed you hard. Disrespected you. Am I sorry?" I paused, then realized what lay ahead. There was nothing to be gained by lying.

"Stop your complaining," I said silently to Cuthbert. "There's a war going on, for Christ's sake, and each of us needs to do our part."

My thoughts then gave way to a quiet calculation, the same one I used with each of my agents, but now it was Cuthbert's turn. Would he betray me? Reveal me to the gestapo? How far could I push my wooden nemesis before he aggravated my limp and exposed me as *la dame qui boite*? But resting him was a risk. No. I'd roll the dice and place my hopes on the doctor's balm. I shut the door on Cuthbert and forced him from my mind.

Hidden from below, I turned my attention to the pace of prison life: men in ill-fitting garb shuffled listlessly, mingling with others around smoky fires, their arms wrapped tightly around themselves on this overcast spring day. The buildings looked like heavily fortified chicken coops—two rows of ten whitewashed barracks, jammed together side by side, each with high horizontal slits for windows.

Its defenses were formidable. Twin barbed wire fences separated by ten yards of dirt were topped with circular bands of razor wire, and the guard towers at the corners had line-of-sight along the entire boundary. Two sets of armed guards with dogs moved briskly through the yard, making their rounds, inspecting the fence, and roughing up prisoners for no apparent reason.

I looked at my watch as the guards moved about the camp and concluded the five Corsicans had seven to nine minutes to escape their locked barracks, break through the two fences, and flee into the forest.

*   *   *

We had cabbage for dinner that night, and by the light of a wood fire in Gaby Bloch's sparsely furnished kitchen, she told me what she'd learned. The light flickered in the dark, illuminating half her face.

"The man, Noble, shares the room with my husband and is working on a plan, but he needs many things. Money, tools, and drugs to make someone ill." She spoke with an upturned voice, which made her list sound like a question.

I nodded. "Yes. But how will you get all of this to Noble?"

"I've used what little money I have to bribe the guards to bring in forbidden items. But," Gaby said angrily, "within the walls of Mauzac, there are snitches who will do anything for an extra ration. One man, Marcel Fleuret, was brought into the plan but has grown fearful and has declared himself opposed to the escape." She paused, then said ruefully, "And my husband says there are not five men who must escape; there are eleven."

JULY 1942, MAUZAC PRISON

At three o'clock in the morning, July 15, I was behind the wheel of a battered Citroen truck. Gaby Bloch, beside me, was nervously twirling her straight brown hair with two fingers. Waiting in the stillness of that late hour reminded me of my early days driving a clumsy medical van with the French Ambulance Service. Anxious for the call, not for prisoners but for the dead and dying at the front. There was an eerie calm there, too, the same thick mixture of anticipation and dread.

The hours of complete darkness were a secret time. No one had a right to be there and once you enter it, you felt like a thief. And this time it was true: we were trespassers, stealing what the guards, with their guns, vowed to keep. The watchtowers' spotlights, trained on the fence, were searching for burglars just like us.

Silently, we ran through the escape plan in our minds. It was a good plan, organized and executed the best it could be. Tools had been provided, money had been smuggled in, the drug Gaby wanted, dissolved in a liquid, ready to drink. Still, so many details. The smallest one could trip us up.

At precisely 3:10 a.m., the door to the Corsicans' barracks open slowly. Just a crack. We had timed the guards, and that night two groups of two circled the perimeter fence every sixteen minutes— leaving just eight minutes for the escape. The first group had just stopped in front of the barracks door, which closed quietly. They lit a pair of cigarettes. The orange glowed bright for a second, and white smoke curled upward. The soldiers lingered, laughed, turned, and returned their slow walk.

They continued their stroll, stopping occasionally to look around and jiggle door handles. Several times they peered into the woods up as if they heard something coming from our direction, but we were silent, dressed in black, our faces streaked with grease. The guards passed.

The door opened again, slowly. The eleven Corsicans had barely enough time to get through two fences unobserved before the next set of guards returned.

One silhouette moved toward the fence and struggled mightily to pull up the bottom strands of barbed wire that had loosened from the post. The cords still seemed taught so he pushed the post back and forth again and again, then lifted the wire one more time. Precious seconds were slipping away. A sawhorse emerged from the barracks and was slid under the wire with what appeared to be cardboard placed nearby. This silent drama was on the edge of the light. Maybe the sentries were playing cards or dozing. Who knew? But they might look up at any moment.

The first prisoner struggled under the wire, crossed the dirt strip, and approached the next fence. I looked at my watch. Five minutes had elapsed, longer than any of us had expected, and the second group of guards soon would be rounding the corner on their return trip. Gaby tugged her locks.

The silhouette lifted the next fence with a board then returned to the first fence. There he motioned to the barracks, and the first shadows slipped, one by one, underneath the wire—one departure every fifteen seconds. Seven minutes passed and barely half the Corsicans had made it through. With time counting down, five more needed to escape, and in a desperate move, they rushed to the fence as a group, and two by two wriggled under the barbed wire.

The guards were at the corner and stopped. Two cupped hands, an orange flame, and a wisp of smoke as one more shadow emerged from the barracks. A twelfth man.

The guards continued around the corner, their heads seemed

focused on the barracks and not toward the scene still unfolding just outside of the lights: the saw horse and cardboard being removed and the last man drifting into the darkness.

As the men climbed into the back of the van, Jean-Pierre hoisted himself into the cab. He embraced Gaby with as much vigor as a man who'd served hard time in prison could muster. She was right—his face was narrow and drawn, but now the corners of his mouth curled upward in weak satisfaction.

I drove the Citroen down the dirt road as planned, toward Villamblard, and eavesdropped on Gaby's conversation with Jean Pierre.

"Noble was the leader," Jean-Pierre said. "He created the plan, made the key, and greased the door to ease our escape."

"And the medicine?" Gaby asked.

"Fleuret was relegated to the clinic and had no ability to interfere."

Several minutes passed. Jean-Pierre was beginning to relax, his head tilted back and wagging to the motion of the truck over the bumps and divots in the gravel road. His eyes were slits, but I couldn't resist a small question.

"And the guard in the tower. Was he asleep?"

Jean-Pierre pulled his head forward and smiled.

"Guards are not well paid. But you can ask him yourself. Sevilla's the twelfth man in the back of the truck."

I had *carte d'identities* for all—except Sevilla—and we dropped him off at the train station. The sun was on the horizon as we passed through the small village of Villamblard, and I pulled off the country road and let the Corsicans escape into the woods. They hid in a nearby abandoned farm for two weeks until the search was called off.

I'd see them again as they filtered into Lyon in ones and twos. Doctor Rousset provided medical assistance, and all became wards in his asylum for the mentally ill. There they stayed, unobserved and recuperating, until SOE agent Vic Gerson, who established exfiltration routes for downed airmen, stopped by with one of his agents. The Corsicans were divided into two groups, and after the men were strong enough, Vic led them on the grueling trek through the Pyrenees to freedom in Spain. Within a few weeks all were safe in London.

MAY 1942, LYON

We'd heard bits and pieces over the wireless. Mysterious chatter about an Allied operation called Jubilee planned for the coast of France. Gloria's stream of intelligence from its spies in the German navy was in high demand. It seemed Jerry was building blockhouses and machine gun nests, moving military units, and fortifying its defenses along a rocky stretch of beach on the coast of Normandy.

London stayed mum about the details but since I'd become a link in the chain of intelligence reporting, I had ideas about what the Allies had planned. After Lucas from Autogiro went missing, his brother Gauthier, the railway man, picked up Gloria's reports on his runs north, sifted through the gossip and fact, and he passed the best of what he had to me. I sent it off to London. The chain, Gloria to Ventriloquist to Heckler to London, stayed strong.

Until it broke.

Heckler received an urgent coded message from London:

```
Gauthier arrested in Issodoun. London's
link with Gloria must be mended at all
cost. Buck
```

In an instant, Gauthier's Ventriloquist circuit was gone, and London's tenuous connection with Gloria was ripped apart yet again. Now, without Ventriloquist, Heckler would forge the link between Gloria and London. I'd be travelling to into the German Occupied Zone to regain London's contact.

The muscles in my jaw tensed and I snapped at Gregoire. Circuits were collapsing all around. Hundreds of agents went missing, most went underground, but many, too, were dead. As callous as it sounds, I was never attentive to battlefield deaths. Why? They were gone. Off the board. What kept me up at night were those who were alive, and in return for life, had been turned by the gestapo into double agents ready to sell us out. And now it was up to me to sort through it all, and clean up this goddam mess.

It was a high-stakes poker game. All of London's cards for France were on the table. So many circuits—Interallied, Autogiro, and now Ventriloquist—penetrated or burned. A wrong move in the Occupied Zone and Heckler would be gone, too, leaving London deaf and blind to what was happening in France. But London was hungry for whatever Gloria could deliver. Operation Jubilee was too important.

It was set. I'd meet Gloria's leader, Jeanine Picabia in Paris.

*   *   *

I patted the breast pocket of my cotton jacket, which held my *carte d'identitè* neatly inscribed with the name Brigitte LeContre but feared my quickly concocted cover story too flimsy. The phony letter from my invented sister, Simone, in my purse, inviting me for a visit, was all I had. No backup in Paris to support my story. Very thin ice, indeed. If the gestapo stopped me and dug deeper for Simone, my lie would unravel faster than wet spaghetti on a fork.

But this ruse was the lesser of my worries. I had a second *carte d'identitè* in the hip pocket of my plaid skirt bearing the name Virginia Hall.

SOE rules forbid carrying two sets of credentials—if discovered with both sets, I'd be interrogated, if not shot on the spot for espionage. But it was a risk I had to take. The Frenchwoman Brigitte LeContre could be stopped and pass unnoticed in the OZ but the American, Virginia Hall, could not. She'd be hauled off to Gestapo headquarters, and in quick order revealed as the *la dame qui boite*. But credentials bearing the name Virginia Hall would be useful in the Unoccupied Zone. I'd be carrying intelligence reports from Gloria back through Vichy, and if caught, my cover as an American newswoman might afford a shred of credibility, maybe enough for Ambassador Leahy to use to in my defense.

Usually, I can maintain mental discipline and push aside the worst thoughts of what might happen. But I confess, the time leading up to my departure for Paris was punctuated with images of Barbie's cruelty and Albert's public display in Place Belecour. Each time these damaging thoughts arrived I challenged myself: This was prudent risk, I'd say. The Gestapo didn't frequent the slowest train of the day— what the locals called "le train lait"—while in the unoccupied zone.

The time had come and for now, I rested my head lightly on the compartment's dust-streaked window, certain there was time to nap before reaching the border. The gentle rocking of the compartment and the sun's rays on the crown of my head and back of my neck was so soothing.

I was not one to worry when the curtain rises, and could clear my mind when not immediately engaged, so my thoughts began to wander, then fix on comforting thoughts: Cuthbert was behaving; the ointment Rousset prescribed seemed to be working. Mother was safe and secure back at Box Horn, receiving my salary. And now I was in the sun. Warm. For the moment, I was content and drifted off.

It was a sound sleep but I woke with a start. Groggy and annoyed, I lifted my head from the window. Where were those shouts coming from?

All the passengers were gone from my compartment, and the commotion seemed to be coming the head of the car. At first I ignored the racket, thinking it was a couple arguing, but then the shouts grew louder, closer, insistent. Then the unmistakable demand for identity papers. It hit me like a punch to the stomach—even before reaching the border, the gestapo had come aboard and had begun a compartment by compartment search. I hadn't counted on a sweep before the border. The voices were almost upon me.

"Where are your papers? Give them to me. Stand up. Open your coat. Empty your pockets." The authorities were barking orders at passengers and seemed to be closely scrutinizing their documents. I squirmed in my seat, trying desperately to compose myself. My temples now were moist. Too late to destroy my documents. My face felt hot. I only had a minute or two before it was my turn to be searched.

When the gestapo arrived, they found me reading *Gone with the Wind*. The officer barked out his orders. I looked up with innocent eyes and gave the tall, muscular young man with a tight, angry face, my *carte d'identitè*. I smiled. Brigitte LeContre. He demanded my jacket, on seat beside me, but didn't wait. He'd grabbed it, turned the pockets inside out, and demanded I do the same for my skirt. Seated, I complied and by the time he'd returned my jumbled coat, I'd already returned to my book.

My invented preoccupation probably annoyed him. Maybe that's why he was a persistent inquisitor and demanded that I stand. I handed him my handbag and as he was rummaging through it intently, I stood up as gracefully as I could by pulling myself up using the edge of the window, which I leaned against. Standing, I assured the man there were no more pockets to check. Everything was in order. My voice was a little dry, and he didn't seem to notice I was wobbling. Nor, thank God, did he see Cuthbert's straps dangling under my long skirt. No, the gestapo officer was in a hurry, and I was wasting his time. He turned and slammed the compartment door shut.

LATE MAY 1942, PARIS

I'd met Jeanine Picabia, leader of the Gloria circuit, when she was a nurse with France's ninth artillery battalion. It was just as the war had started—before I'd fled Paris for London. Jeanine had joined me several times in my ambulance, and together, we shuttled the wounded between the front and the doctors in Metz. I didn't remember her all that well. My greatest impression was that she had a youthful appearance and smelled fresh, like the outdoors.

I gave the special knock at the door of 11 Rue Chateaubriand in Paris, two strong and one light, and offered the password when it opened a crack. Jeanine ushered me into her apartment with high ceilings. It was a relaxed space; her father's artwork, splashes of blues and reds, hung on the white walls near the arched windows, which bathed the room in light. As we stood, exchanging a few memories of our days in Metz, she pointed to a threadbare chair and invited me to sit.

Jeanine took the chair opposite mine, separated by the window. She still appeared younger than anyone had a right to be and told her so. Despite all she had seen and experienced—the carnage and stress of the intervening years—there were no lines, no gray hairs, no bags under her eyes from sleepless nights. She retained an open and delicate face, her straight, chin-length chestnut hair was pushed over and behind her ears.

Jeanine spoke calmly, but there was an unmistakable edge to her words, which she seemed to choose carefully. Gloria needed help. Without the brothers Lucas and Gauthier to courier information, her circuit was dead in the water, and London was blind and deaf to what was happening on the Normandy coast.

She then confirmed that Lucas had been betrayed by a double agent, the woman in Interallied called Le Chatte. Lucas had taken a gamble and lost.

"Interallied was the first and led to the downfall of others. All because of that Polish bastard, Armand," Jeanine said angrily. She looked out the window, seemingly preoccupied with what might be outside. "Over eighty agents arrested and tortured for their information. Of course, these men have knowledge of our network and yours in Lyon. But we do not know how much they have given up."

"We thought Le Chatte was bad, but London still is receiving transmissions from Interallied. What about its radio?" I asked.

"It is a hollow circuit, controlled by the Germans. Interallied's pianist chose to cooperate, and now the circuit is being played back to London. SOE doesn't know the wireless messages it receives are coming directly from German military intelligence." Jeanine looked disgusted when she said, "I hear London is sending supplies and men to locations where Nazis are waiting to pick them up. Lucas was going to report this, but then he was arrested."

"What circuits are still active?" I asked

"Autogiro is burned, rumors are that Prosper in Paris has been infiltrated," Jeanine said.

"Carte in the south is gone," I said. "Ventriloquist is down now that Gauthier has been jailed." My head was spinning. "Goddammit. Beside Urchin in Marseilles, who's left?"

"The only ones who can help London are Gloria and Heckler,"

Jeanine said, looking away. "But only God knows for how long. We have no choice but to work together. I have fresh information on German plans and defenses around Dieppe but have not been able to report it. My agents collect their information on scraps of paper. I put them in order on one sheet and create maps and charts. Then I bring all of it to a Greek on Avenue Rene Coty, a photographer for Gloria, who reduces it to microdots unreadable to the eye."

"Give me the information and we'll set up a courier schedule for London," I said.

"Jacques Legrand has had luck crossing the line, and my mother, too. Madame Picabia is a very respectable older woman, who conceals these microdots in matchboxes in her pocket or in newspapers rolled up in her shopping bag like she is going to market. She gets up at five o'clock in the morning, fetches a bag from the café near the Gare du Nord and has taken these documents to Autogiro. And," her voice softened but then revived, "she has been successful. Only once did a young gestapo officer question her while waiting for the last train to Paris. But now she is old and no longer has the strength, so we used the abbe—Abbe Alesh—as a courier to Autogiro."

I tensed. Alesh was their courier too. Was I the only one who had questions about the abbe? His name kept popping up wherever there was trouble.

"Tell me about the abbe," I said. "London says he's clean. But I don't believe it."

"Jacques brought Alesh into our organization, and Gloria has not been burned like the others. He is with us now, a man of the cloth, so how could he not be clean? Alesh has offered safe haven to many of our agents who get into trouble with the secret police. The abbe has been good to us. Reliable. I have no reason to believe he is a Judas priest."

No one else questioned the abbe's loyalty. He passed through the lines so easily, but there were too many coincidences. And now with circuits collapsing, he'd be relied on even more. Fewer questions would be asked of a priest.

"I don't trust the abbe," I said flatly. "Use Jacques, use your mother." I said. "Don't use the abbe."

"I will consider what you say. But I have few couriers who get through the line so easily as the priest. Madame Picabia and maybe Jacques can make the trips, but Jacques and I handle a hundred agents."

Gloria was in a bind, and with London desperate for the information, the information had to get to Heckler quickly. We agreed to a twice-a-month courier schedule. When I got up to leave, Jeanine asked if I'd encountered any difficulty crossing into the German occupied zone. I gave a wry laugh, then admitted to traveling with two sets of documents. "Then the gestapo entered my compartment and searched me."

She shook her head and said, "Well sometimes these things cannot be helped. And how did you escape?"

I patted Cuthbert.

"He's hollow, you know. Lately, he's been a pain in the ass, but he treated me kindly today. You'd be surprised what I keep in Cuthbert. He's a regular letterbox."

CHAPTER ELEVEN

———

The Germans flattered me with complements that were undeserved.
They admired my knowledge of languages, my psychological finesse,
even my innate sense of adventure. This new occupation took
advantage of a weak spot in my soul of which
I had previously been unaware.

ABBE ROBERT ALESCH

AUGUST 1942, LYON

August was shaping up to be a dreadful month, my worst since arriving in France. Poor Gregoire, my lifeline to London, spent most of his days darting from safe house to safe house, staying a few steps ahead of German direction-finding vans. He didn't complain either, even though he had every right to, when new DF aircraft began buzzing overhead. My wily pianist could take care of himself. He was the least of my troubles.

I sent a series of short messages to London about Interallied—confirming it was burned and its radio was controlled. I hoped the Polish government in exile could salvage what remained of its network and that London could feed German military intelligence some delicious lies to flush its agents from the shadows or at least have them chase their own tail for a while. This cat and mouse would go on until the Germans caught on to London's scheme.

For the past three months, I had been the middleman between Gloria and London. Jacques Legrand made twice-a-month trips to Lyon to drop off microfilmed documents on the German Navy's activities on the coast of Normandy, but it was London calling the shots, telling Gloria what it wanted, and their demands grew more detailed as the days rolled by.

Over a Cinzano one afternoon, Jacques, the outgoing Frenchman, tall with dark hair and an aggressive nose like a toucan's beak, spoke of Gloria's intelligence network, which worked the coast from Dunkerque to Cherbourg. I smiled when Jacques said he was just a minion and Jeanine was the brains of the operation. She was the one who made sense of it all, adding the larger perspective, then passed the package to Jacques for delivery to Heckler.

It was early June when Jacques' visit turned serious. He said London's demands for Operation Jubilee were more detailed and difficult for his spies to answer. They asked about the slope of the beach and its composition. How about the elevation of the surrounding terrain? Obstructions in the water? So many questions. But what London wanted most, Jacques said, was the most difficult to obtain—photographs, charts of the fortifications, movements of defense personnel. London wanted to know precisely where the Germans were.

I thought Operation Jubilee was a wargame, a dress rehearsal for the large Allied invasion of the continent that everyone knew was coming. I kept my mouth shut about our candid conversations and told Gregoire to do the same when he picked up bits about Jubilee through our daily message traffic. My opinion, though I didn't express it to anyone other than Jacques, was that it was too early, far too early, for an extravagant Allied adventure. Good God, this was the summer of 1942, and Americans had just joined the fight. If the Allies were expecting a resistance force behind the lines to soften up German defenses to support an all-out invasion, well, let's just say it was too soon and leave it at that. When the invasion of Europe did come, the French resistance would need more support, more weapons and warning of Allied intentions to weaken German supply lines before we could hope to prevail. To my way of thinking, the information from

Gloria was important for the big all-out invasion of the continent to come later.

I enjoyed the affable Jacques Legrand with the Gary Cooper twinkle in his eye and nasal tone in his shy voice. I didn't always see him when he made the drop, but when our paths crossed in Dr. Rousset's office, Legrand always had something irreverent to say about London or the peculiar peccadillos of the German soldiers he turned into informants. He was such good fun. But then, inexplicably, his visits stopped in early July and his reporting tailed off, too. Then I found a note in the doctor's letterbox. Jacques said he was now too busy to continue playing courier. Jeanine's mother, Madame Picabia, would bring the information across the line.

Still, it bothered me that the note was so abrupt. It was unlike the good-natured Frenchman to be anything other than sociable. But what concerned me most was the information that came in the twice-monthly drops in the Rousset's letterbox. After Jacques passed the baton to Madame Picabia, the volume and quality of the reporting, well, it just wasn't up to standards. Fewer reports of any length or depth. Less timely information. Few if any micro photographs. It was as if the spigot to the information was slowly being turned off.

That got me to thinking about the conversation Jeanine and I had said in her apartment, that circuits were collapsing all around. Inter-allied, gone. Autogiro, disbanded. Ventriloquist without Gauthier? As good as dead. Now, having unraveled the major circuits in occupied France, had the gestapo trained its sights on Gloria?

I couldn't let it rest. Gloria knew much about Heckler. Working so closely, our fates were intertwined. I radioed London with my concerns, and they offered a one-line response: they'd look into it.

That was just the first week of that most dreadful month.

The third week of August, the fifteenth to be exact, a truly horrible picture began to emerge. I remember that date because of my violent reaction to opening the *Le Monde* that morning. I wanted to throw up. The banner headline read:

Allied Attack on Dieppe Ends in Rout.

An expeditionary force of six thousand troops had landed on the beach of Dieppe with a mission to occupy, destroy, and then withdraw from the port. Ironically, the newspaper said the operation was to be a show of force, prove the Allies' resolve, boost troop morale. Instead, it was a dreadful defeat. It seemed the enemy had been tipped off and was lying in wait for the Allies to come ashore. Then, just when they were most vulnerable, exposed on the beach, the Germans attacked with mortars and machine-gun fire, and they pinned our boys against the cliff of that rocky coast. They didn't stand a chance. The narrow beach face became a killing field. When it was over, thousands of mostly Canadian troops lay dead or wounded, washed up with the tide. Thousands more were captured. I rolled up the paper and threw it to the ground. I couldn't read more.

Gloria somehow was wrapped up in this ghastly failure.

My answer from London came quickly and confirmed that the circuit had collapsed and though SOE couldn't be sure, it suspected Jeanine had escaped and was on the run—most likely on her way to the Pyrenees via Lyon.

I was prepared for a late-night knock at the door, and it came two days later around two a.m. My first reaction to an unexpected knock is always to check the window. No Black Marias at the curb. I made my way to the door and opened it just a crack. It was Jeanine.

"For God's sake," she said in a low voice, "let me in."

Jeanine pushed past me, out of breath, and had a wild look: disheveled hair, rumpled clothing, stooped shoulders. So different from last time. For a moment, we only spoke with our eyes, but that was long enough to see her pain and worry. I didn't ask for the password, and she was in no mood to give it. I quickly closed the door.

She threw her tweed jacket on the living room chair. Her eyes shifted to the floor and seemed fixed on my tattered oriental runner. Her young face was flushed and her forehead wrinkled as she began to pace, deep in thought, no doubt racing through the rooms of her mind, trying to make sense of recent events and planning her next steps.

Still panting, she said, "Jacques was picked up last Friday, and now the gestapo is rolling up the rest of our assets. Gloria is burned."

I wasn't ready to hear her story. Not yet. I wanted assurance that we were safe, that she hadn't been tailed. I went again to the margin of the window. "You did a surveillance detection route before showing up at my door, right?"

"Yes. Yes, of course," she said irritated. "I lost my tail, one from the secret police, before I boarded the train."

Hiding my face again, I slowly moved one eye to the border of the glass, looked through the sheer white curtain to the rain-soaked boulevard below. Under the narrow beam of the streetlight, a German officer had his arm around a woman of the street. The secret police and gestapo were more heavy-handed, I thought. No one loitering. No cars or henchmen waiting by the curb. We were safe for now.

My words flew in short, low bursts. Jeanine, as a leader of Gloria, bore some responsibility for the network's demise. "All right," I said, staring at her, "Where's Jacques?"

"I spent a week out in Normandy visiting agents. I was returning, two blocks from our safe house in Paris, when I saw Jacques being led away in handcuffs. Just before the gestapo pushed him into the back seat of a Black Maria, our eyes met and I saw his warning. I felt so useless. All I could do was turn and walk away. I knew then that Gloria was lost.

"My mother said Jacques was taken to Fresnes for interrogation, where the gestapo beat him without mercy. Our contacts in the prison said his head was plunged into a bathtub filled with ice water until he passed out." Jeanine pushed her right hand over her forehead and through her tangled mane. Her face hung low toward the ground. Her voice cracked. "He was thrown to the floor, unconscious, and beaten savagely. Blood was everywhere. Jacques' skull was nearly crushed under the gestapo's boot." She looked toward the window, perhaps to gather the courage to continue. "My partner was barely alive when he was loaded onto the train bound for Buchenwald."

"And your agents. What about the rest of Gloria?"

"Jacques was the first. The rest?" Jeanine let out a sigh. "I don't know."

Jeanine seemed to be aging before my eyes. Now slumping in my living room chair, gone was her innocence. Her open face was now lined in worry, and her black hair, disheveled, hung over her forehead and ears and looked like it hadn't been combed for days. "I'm struggling trying to understand," she said. "All of that information we collected for so long, all of our agents working so hard. All those questions from London that we answered. All of it for nothing."

The heat had settled in my chest where it formed a hard knot. Maybe it was because my friend Jacques Legrand was taken or because Gloria was burned and Heckler now was at risk. But at that moment, it was because Gloria had failed at Dieppe. Our eyes roamed the room. Not on each other. Jeanine and I were miles apart, and I was struggling to understand how it all fell to pieces.

"We gave Heckler all the information," said Jeanine, "the documents from our sources in the German military. On the bunkers. The battalions moving forward. The photographs. You saw it. You sent it to London, right?"

"Listen, Jeanine," I said in disgust, walking away from the window. "After Jacques stopped coming in July, your reporting lost its edge. It was anemic. You knew how important Operation Jubilee was. London expected more from you, and I did too, but you didn't deliver."

Jeanine blew up. "Goddammit! We sent everything we could. Our best agents worked on this for months. Dozens of microfilm photographs, bunkers ringing the cliffs, the dangers on the beach, dossiers on battery commanders, information on troop movements, all of it. We had Jubilee tied down five different ways."

I didn't believe Jeanine. "We saw nothing of the sort."

Fuming, I lurched to my bedroom as fast as Cuthbert would allow, to retrieve my stash of documents. I sat down in my bedside chair, leaned over, threw back the carpet, and yanked up the floorboard that hid my secret trove. Leaving it all in a jumbled mess, I hobbled back to Jeanine, who was waiting in the kitchen.

"Here," I said, throwing the manila folder on the table. "Here's a copy of your goddam file. All the information I received for the past two months. Look for yourself. What you provided was worthless. No film. No reports of value. Nothing. It was pitiful."

Jeanine rifled through the pages. "This can't be all of it," she said.

Where are the photos? The hand-drawn maps?" Her eyes, unblinking and unbelieving, fixed on the folder. Then she looked up and her face grew crimson.

My face tightened. "That's all you gave Heckler. All of it."

Jeanine stood, lifted the file up above her head and threw it on the table. The papers scattered to the wooden floor below. "Goddammit! Damn it to hell! This isn't a fraction of what we gave you."

I exploded. "Well, then," I said, "Where's the rest of it? How . . . Who had access to this file? Who was the courier? You said your mother was making the drop."

"No," Jeanine said. She turned quiet, bowed her head and shook it slowly. "It wasn't Mother. It was the abbe. Alesh was the courier."

"Goddammit!," I said. "I told you not to use the priest!"

With Gloria now in tatters, there was nothing more to be said. The fog had lifted and we saw the final pieces that had fallen into place. The enemy had been with us all along and the gestapo understood all of it—the people, relationships between circuits, and the agents—and now they were closing in.

I had known Alesh was phony. While the others had embraced him, I'd pushed him aside. London insisted he was clean; Doctor Rousset vouched for the abbe, saying he was a good Gaulist; and those who worked closest with Alesh believed a priest incapable of betrayal. Everyone had been duped, including SOE.

I blamed myself. For the longest time, I'd been willing to be swayed by de Guelis, MI-6 and all the rest. The agent roll-ups, the cascading collapse of other networks leading to Gloria. Alesh was the common thread that tied these defeats together.

I tossed and turned the remainder of the night, thinking about the next moves. My agents should go into hiding, immediately. Most of all, Madame Guerin, who offered food and shelter, and Dr. Rousset, whose office was a meeting place for agents and the letterbox for Gloria's messages to Heckler.

Early the next morning, I rushed to Rousset's office. Strangely, as I neared his office, he appeared, running toward me. The doctor waved his arms wildly and shouted for to meet him in his office quickly. I ran as fast as Cuthbert would allow and arrived breathless. My hands on my knees, I looked up and tried forming words, but nothing came out. Rousset, excitedly, beat me to the first sentence, and ushered me into the backroom for a secret conversation.

I rose and limped toward the closed door. My face, flushed, felt a little rush of wind as he opened it. A man standing in the corner with his back toward me had a familiar outline. The door latch click shut, leaving the two of us in the room.

The man turned around. It was Alesh.

I was stunned. "Bastard," was the first and only word that came out. "You goddam bastard." Then I turned silent to catch my breath. I knew he could see the fire and flame I felt all over my face. "The Lies. Deceit. I could kill you with my bare hands for what you did."

Full of rage, I looked around for a tool, any implement—scissors, a surgical blade. Nothing presented itself, only a doctor's stethoscope on the white metal counter. The rubber tubes. I grabbed it.

The abbe understood. "Listen . . . listen," Alesh said. "Yes. I have sinned grievously, yes, grievously, this I know. And I betrayed many, many."

I moved closer to the abbe, looking for the right angle.

His eyes, intense, held terror. "But, listen . . . please. Listen," he said, pleading. "I still believe. Yes, I still believe. And . . . and I am here to confess. Yes, confess. You need to know what I know. Would it not be better for you to know what I know? And warn others. Yes, then, then, I will surrender my myself to you. Give you my life."

I still was fuming, but something had pierced my anger and made me pause. There was a logic to what the abbe said. I considered his words. Momentum was carrying me forward, but I stopped. "Two minutes," I said.

"At first the gestapo was gentle," Alesh said, sweating profusely. He spoke rapidly. "They knew Albert came to see me. I held out at first. Yes, I was brave. I said, 'I serve as a refuge only.' But then their questions became more angry. Demanding. They said, 'No you are an accomplice, a conspirator.' They told me their case. I had been trailed for some time. They said, 'Now is the time to pull in the net and catch the fish. We don't usually interview priests but you are a special case.'"

The abbe put his finger between his neck and collar, wanting air. "The gestapo said, 'We can talk here, or we can take you into the back room to visit Doctor Barbie. If you decide to see the doctor, you should prepare yourself for a painful departure to the hereafter.' To the hereafter, Germaine, the hereafter."

The abbe broke down. "I am feeble and pathetic," he said tearfully. "I should place my full trust in God, but I was given a choice of life or a painful death. I should not be fearful, but I was not ready to see the face of my Creator. I chose life. I now know that was wrong, when so many suffered for my sins. But what came next, I acted without a conscience. And so my sins became compounded. I was a Judas, then it was a small step from receiving life to receiving pieces of silver and their flattery, which soothed my fears and insecurities.

"But I have come to confess my sins now. A small step, yes. But my confession can save your life. I come to you now because the gestapo knows of your work in Mauzac, your connections to Autogiro and Gloria and British agents. They know you have saved many of your countrymen, and now the gestapo is putting up posters around Lyon with your face. They call you the most dangerous Allied agent in all of France, and Herr Barbie says he must catch you. Yes, I admit that I betrayed others to save myself. But I did not betray you. I confess now so you may escape. The gestapo knows where you live. I did not tell them this; they learned it through the collapse of Gloria. They may be watching.

"Now I have confessed and am ready to surrender myself to you and to God. But please, do it quickly. Then you must escape."

Killing the abbe. It felt right. Deserved for all the death he had caused on the beaches of Dieppe, the round-ups of agents, the destruction of British networks. Our instructors back at Beaulieu had said that killing was a last resort. "Use it," they said, "when every other option fails."

But I had an idea. One last option. I let the abbe go. He was forever grateful, but I wasn't through with him.

That night, I sent message in a code that could easily be broken on the controlled frequency used by Interallied. It was short. It said that Abbe Alesh, the double agent, had been turned and again was offering his services to Heckler. As my pianist Gregoire hit the last key, I wondered how long it would take the gestapo to pick up the abbe and begin a new round of painful interrogation.

CHAPTER TWELVE

―――――――

My address has been given to Vichy. My time is about up.
VIRGINIA HALL

NOVEMBER 1942, PERPIGNAN, FRANCE

I caught the last train from Lyon, the eleven p.m., and arrived early
the next morning in Perpignan, a city of narrow cobblestone streets,
terracotta roofs, and an imposing red stone castle overlooking the
glacier-capped Pyrenees. This thirteenth century city had become a
Vichy no-man's-land, filling with the desperate, each waiting their
turn, willing to lose it all on the rugged mountain trails leading to
freedom in Spain. Now I was one of the desperate too.

Returning to Perpignan after fifteen months, I was more irritated
than sentimental, though I hadn't given much thought to my own
escape until it became inevitable. I had unfinished business, so I
stayed in Lyon as long as I could, but my residence was known to
authorities, and it seemed I spent most of my time shuttling back and
forth between safe houses, dodging the gestapo. But then news and
events started stacking up like cards in a bad hand of poker, and my

luck had run out. I could feel the breath of gestapo chief Klaus Barbie on my neck. I saw the posters in Lyon offering a reward for *La Dame Qui Boite*, but the last straw was the warning from French agents loyal to de Gaulle: German soldiers, fresh from defeat in North Africa, would begin flooding into Lyon. The veil that was Vichy, the tissue covering Nazi control over the Unoccupied Zone, would be ripped off, and Barbie could blanket the city to conduct a house-to-house search for the lady with a limp.

That final warning from French agents came much too quickly; German soldiers were on their way, and I had just one hour to prepare for a hasty departure. It would be a race to the border, which soon would be sealed. I was frantic, preoccupied with closing Heckler—burning codebooks and documents—and then dashing off. I'm ashamed to say that my agents were an afterthought. There was little time to give them warning, offer money, and show them a way out. The gestapo was coming.

Just after boarding the late-night train in Lyon, that sinking emptiness arrived when I had time to consider those left behind. Madame Guerin and Dr. Rousset. I told myself not to imagine what might happen, not to speculate on the tools the Gestapo might use to make them talk, not to think about the agony painted on their face as they were tortured, and not to dwell on whether they might die a painful death merely because they had known and helped me. After they talked—and they would talk—the circle would expand to others on the fringe of Heckler. The Labouriers with their trucks, the Joulians with their factory printing press, Madame Catin, my courier, and all the others.

Is it too harsh to say I abandoned my agents? No. It isn't. But there were reasons beyond my control. That's what I told myself. The Brits and Americans had a war to win, and all of us had our roles to play. My agents had their lives in France, and I was a stranger helping them realize their dreams of freedom, offering an organization, some support, and a way to bring their long nightmare to an end. And I had no time. The end came too soon. I couldn't protect them, but I couldn't deny that their voices lingered in my thoughts. I tried to hold them at bay, but these feelings lingered, and their faces, fixed in my mind.

Before catching the last train to Perpignan, I packed a few items hurriedly. Clothing, of course, that Guerin had given me for men passing through the Haute Loire. I didn't have much to choose from: heavy wool trousers, a shirt, boots, gloves, a hat, an overcoat—all in men's sizes, dreadfully heavy and much too large. I added a stump sock, Noxzema, and a few personal items. As a final act, I handed Gregoire a message for London, his last transmission before he shut it all down. He tapped out on his piano:

Dindy's first tooth nearly visible.

That was all. Then he unplugged the wireless and packed it up. London would forward the short message to the Barcelona consulate. I was on my way. I left Lyon. Heckler was closed.

The Pyrenees—my only choice. The Gestapo was closing in, and all other avenues of escape were sealed. I wanted a covert departure by trawler from Marseilles—it would have been a much easier trip—but the Nazi retreat from North Africa made that impossible, and now the port was positively swarming with Germans. The full coast of the Mediterranean clear to Gibraltar was filled with Nazi warships and coastal patrol boats.

It was overcast the Thursday I arrived in Perpignan at the foot of the Pyrenees. The clouds, low and diffuse, moved quickly like cannon smoke and piled up in the south, forming roiling columns like angry sentinels waiting above the rocky slopes. The signs were unmistakable and all around me. The sun, low in the sky, the dampness in the air, the frigid north wind against my cheek: winter had arrived in the mountains. Cuthbert would have to be on his best behavior to get us through this, but he couldn't stay silent on that rocky, frozen trail. My stomach churned. I had to get on with it.

I followed the same instructions I'd given many times before to desperate agents and airmen passing through Lyon. Gilbert could be found by the ornate fountain of winged victory at the end of Rue de la Republic a few minutes after two p.m. And that's where I met him. London tipped the Frenchman to expect me, and after catching his attention, I motioned to an adjacent alley between two gray concrete buildings. He arrived a few minutes later.

Gilbert was not the kind of man I thought he'd be. Short and round, he wore a black beret, dirty brown trousers pulled high above his bulging waist, and a gray wool jacket requiring yards of material that barely covered his rawhide belt. His round face, unshaven for several days, was deeply tanned and highlighted a speck of white spittle trapped in the left corner of his mouth. He smelled of burnt tobacco and cheap wine.

Gilbert didn't seem fit enough to cross the Pyrenees, but then he didn't have to be. He was a businessman, the planner, much like a prize-fight promoter, in the business but a spectator of the sport. He stayed behind the scenes, matching *passeurs* who followed the narrow, little-known rock and dirt paths winding through the jagged cliffs with what he called his "clients." It was a job that demanded street smarts and discretion and a record of bringing men safely over the mountains. I expected him to do the same for me.

"So, Germaine," Gilbert said, "after sending me many clients, we finally meet but you chose a most dangerous time for your first visit," he said. "The city is filling with the despairing, and the enemy is in pursuit. For anyone looking to exit France before the door closes, it will be a race to the border." He looked skyward, and his expression soured. "And this weather. I am not sure who benefits more from a storm. The hare or the hound."

"I regret all of my best *passeurs* are busy with other clients or engaged in commercial enterprises. These are good times for guides willing to take the risk. But I do have one man, Germaine, only one. Miguel. He knows the way, but like many whose profession is trafficking in forbidden items, well, he has, shall we say, some rough edges.

Gilbert hesitated briefly and stoked the stubble on his chin, as if in thought on how to proceed. "He says he does not take women on the trail. Too much trouble. Too slow, he says. But I said, 'Miguel. Look. Germaine has been good to me. She will make no trouble.

Make this one exception.' He had set his mind against it and said 'no' many times. But after several bottles of rioja . . ."

"Rough edges," I said, interrupting, "that doesn't bother me. People tell me I have some myself."

"Then it is a good match," Gilbert said with a small laugh. The deal struck, he began to speak rapidly. His attention shifted to the details, and he seemed anxious that we might be seen together.

"Of course, the charge is greater because of the danger. Twenty thousand francs," he said, looking quickly over his left shoulder. Two German soldiers had just entered the alley. He stayed silent until they passed.

"Miguel will be on the bridge over the river Basse by Le Castillet at dusk, and you will leave from there. Bring only what you need for this three-day journey."

I nodded, then extended my hand.

"To say '*bon chance*' brings the possibility of the opposite," Gilbert said, "so all I will say is *until we meet again*."

Miguel arrived at the other end of the stone bridge at dusk just as Gilbert said. I was waiting motionless, my arms draped over the grey granite wall, looking at a leaf floating through the eddies of the Basse, and glanced up in time to see Miguel point a burning cigarette between his fingers toward a battered forest green cargo truck in an alley adjacent to the red castle.

After speaking with Gilbert, I hadn't been able to keep an open mind about my *passeur*, and on seeing Miguel for the first time, my suspicions seemed to be confirmed. He wore the look of disdain on his unshaven face and had the swagger of a scoundrel. Even before he opened his mouth filled with crooked brown teeth, I hated the very idea of placing my life in his hands.

Miguel was a man of small stature, and in the twilight, his light black beard made his face look grubby. I shouldn't have held it against him—all guides are in it for the money—but Miguel seemed more mercenary than most. Gilbert had said that my *passeur* was a republican with no need for Franco or anyone else who didn't have the cash to pay for his services.

The disgust stayed painted on his face as we approached the truck. Just before reaching the hood, he stopped and leaned back. His eyes moved upward: first my feet, then my chest, and finally my eyes. The corners of his mouth stayed downturned as if he had just tasted something most foul. Cuthbert rocked under my pant leg but stayed hidden. I had no intention of revealing him to this man, ever.

"This will be a hard trip," Miguel said, "even for a strong man. But for a woman in a man's clothing?" He shook his head. "I say no." He took a last drag on his cigarette and flicked the butt hard to the ground. As he spoke, smoke escaped his lips. "A woman cannot keep up. In the mountains, survival is not a game. The slow cannot hold back the pace of the fast."

His eyes lingered on the ground, his mouth slightly open, as he crushed the still burning ember with the heel of his boot. Then he looked directly into my eyes. "Woman-in-man's-clothes, you must know now. I will not wait. I will not help. I will leave you in the cold, and you will die. I show you mercy now by telling you this, because the mountains show no mercy."

The mountains were unforgiving, I knew that, but my chances of survival were better climbing the Pyrenees than staying in France. I glared back. I wasn't moved.

He took a step toward me, and his eyes stayed fixed on my chest. "We cannot wait. The mountain passes will soon close."

"I expected snow," I said.

He gave a derisive laugh. "It is not the snow. It is the Germans flooding into Vichy. The trails from Toulouse and St. Girons, the shorter routes, will be the first to close. No, the trail I will take is not yet known. It is long but will not remain secret for many more days.

"There is one more thing," Miguel said, spitting out his words like an epithet. "I do not take women, but if you are so foolish as to come along, you must pay a premium. The cost is 25,000 francs. The full amount now."

"Half now and the rest when we cross the border." Before he could argue, I took out a thick billfold, peeled off 13,000 francs, and placed it in his hands. He appeared startled by how quickly I paid. His eyes followed my billfold as I eased it back into my pocket.

"There are two others in the truck, a man from Australia and another Frenchman. They need to cross but cannot . . .."

"I will pay for them," I said quickly.

"Now," he said impatiently.

"No. Fifteen for both now and fifteen more in Spain. You've seen that I can pay."

Miguel thought for a moment and watched silently as my billfold reemerged. His eyes stayed wide and fixed on the cash being counted on his hand. He stuffed the notes into his pants pocket.

Miguel turned his back and headed toward the cab door. "Throw your pack into the truck," he said. "Your companions are in the hay. There's a blanket. We leave pronto."

The Aussie and Frenchman must have heard us talking because they were at the cargo bay ready to lend a hand. The engine sputtered, the gears engaged, and we bumped into each other awkwardly in the dried grass. I offered a quick greeting and the Frenchman, nervously, asked if I knew the path Miguel would be taking over the Pyrenees. I said we'd be passing through the forbidden zone to the drop off point—that much was certain—but I had no idea where trek would begin.

"Miguel, now he's a piece of work," the Aussie said. "The bastard mumbled something about Col de Tivoli, but God knows where that is." I let the comment rest, but it wasn't on any map I'd seen either. The Frenchman stared at the roof of the truck silently as all of us settled in.

It was about three hours before sunrise when the truck lurched to a stop, and the cab door slammed shut. From the dark came a disinterested mumble from Miguel:

"We start here."

I shook out the cobwebs and pulled hay from my hair. Cuthbert buckled as I lowered myself from the cab, but no one seemed to notice.

Before us, I later learned, was the walled city of Villefranche-de-Conflent. If this were a different time, I might have entered the arched entrance to the city on the banks of the river Caddy. But that early morning, the village was buttoned up, and the thought of a detour was far from my mind.

We stretched, I yawned, and together we started slowly, taking those first tentative steps into the pitch black. Thankfully, Cuthbert was behaving himself, he'd had plenty of rest, but I hadn't a clue how long my wooden companion would stay silent while the rest of my body was under assault by the frigid night air, which splashed my face like a bucket of ice water. Above, a sliver of the moon with an icy halo illuminated high flat clouds that looked like layers of rock. A shiver raced through my body and fed a sense of dread for what lay ahead.

In front, Miguel started walking as if he were late for an appointment, past the city's walls and up a small street that ended by a river. None of us could keep pace.

The Aussie ran up to Miguel and said something I couldn't hear. But then he reached into his pocket and pulled out a white handkerchief and tied it to Miguel's rucksack. Even if we couldn't keep pace, maybe we could see the Spaniard off in the distance.

All of us were well-versed on the rules and kept to them. We'd stay put and sleep during the day, no wandering around on our own, and when the darkness came, we'd walk: stay in line, no talking, and no smoking. A burning ember could be seen for miles. If we were lucky, we'd have some moonlight to show us the way. Tonight would be a short walk. Only a few hours until sunrise.

The trail hugged the river's gentle banks, and even with little illumination, the terrain appeared most agreeable: flat and grassy, with a hard-packed dirt trail. If it hadn't been so damn cold and dark, it would have been a beautiful start. The reassuring rush of water over the rocks masked all sounds. The ancient trees with their knotty trunks bent toward the sky. The moon, though only a thin crescent, glowed through the leafless branches that cast long, arching shadows.

My companions' eyes were fixed on the three feet of ground that lay in front of them, and if the terrain had been uneven, my eyes would have been there too, but the scene drew me in, and for a moment I forgot the challenge that lay ahead. Miguel, that sour pessimist, tried to scare me off me by saying the forecast was for bad weather. Maybe it was true, but at that moment, it didn't bother me.

We were underway, and all of us were getting farther and farther from the gestapo. But it was cold. Damn cold.

I kept up with the group along the banks of the river that we later learned was called the Rotja. The Frenchman followed Miguel and the Aussie was behind me, but soon the trail began to curve upward, and what had been a smooth hard pack path gave way to a rumpled track of embedded rock. The Rotja began to fall away into the ravine.

I began taking deeper breaths. Moisture was forming on my brow. Cuthbert caused a twinge, a small bite to my stump, nothing I could call discomfort yet, but he'd begun to whine.

It wasn't too much later that the eastern horizon turned burnt orange and we were approaching the small village called Py. That evening's walk, Miguel hadn't looked around once to check on us. Now his pace slowed, and he stopped at a barn.

"We stay here," he said, opening the door. He headed for the farthest corner, and the Frenchman followed, leaving the Aussie to share breakfast with me.

We were eating biscuits with raspberry jam, when the Aussie spoke up. "Someday, you'll have to tell me the story about your wooden mate beneath your pant leg."

Startled by his brashness, I craned my neck to see if anyone else was listening. At the far end of the barn, Miguel had wolfed-down his meal and was cleaning his rifle while listening to the Frenchman. The Aussie's comment came upon me so quickly, usually I'm uncomfortable being revealed in any way, but responded in the manner the question came to me, quietly and candidly. On reflection, his willingness to engage me so honestly was refreshing and his voice was barely a whisper. I smiled. I knew he'd keep my secret safe.

"I had an uncle who came back from the Great War with a fake leg that came clear up to his thigh. Lizzy, that's what he called the old girl," he said with a grin. "When he got drunk, he'd take her off, lay it on the bar and tell the story about how he lost his leg in the forests of Verdun. Each time I heard the story, he'd exaggerate a bit more. I was just a young tyke, but by the time he passed, I thought he'd won the war singlehandedly."

I smiled. "My story isn't as interesting. My Cuthbert wasn't earned in such a noble cause. Certainly nothing worthy of embellishment," I told him in a voice intended only for the two of us. "A hunting accident years ago. My own stupidity, really."

"You hide it well. I wouldn't have known, seeing you walk the flat."

"I'll take that as a compliment, but I'm sure in a few more miles, when we really begin to climb, Miguel will happily throw me into a snowdrift and be done with me."

He laughed, then turned silent, looking straight ahead as if I'd triggered a thought.

I suppose I was fishing for some encouragement, some sign of support, but it didn't come.

He turned toward me awkwardly. His right shoulder lacked movement. It seemed immobile.

"My de Havilland got shot up over Toulouse. My 'chute got me down a bit mangled but in one piece, and a doctor in Carcassonne patched me up. My bad luck, going down, but I made a good show of it. Gave it to Fritz good, and I'm in one piece, so no complaints here. Well, they said the trail through St. Girons was getting too hot, so they put me on to Gilbert." He looked down. "But I tell you, our *passeur* has a reputation," the Aussie said. Seeing our Frenchman companion approach, he spoke quickly to finish his thought. "For leaving people in the lurch."

The Frenchman returned with a smile.

"Miguel, he's not so bad. He told me two more days of climbing and hiking. Tomorrow we'll scale Col de Mantet, climb down to a small town, cross a river, then make our way to a cabin, where a partisan will give us shelter. Twenty-five kilometers, he said. The next day will be a little shorter. Seventeen. More of the same, but we make a tricky border-crossing in daylight. Then down to train station at San Juan de las Abadesas, and we're off to Barcelona. A hop, skip, and a jump and we're home."

The Frenchman made it sound effortless. A hop, skip, and a jump. But then he didn't know even these seemingly easy movements would be monumentally difficult for me. The dread for the next few days had begun to well up inside of me, but knowing the broad outlines of our journey gave me some comfort, something to hold onto, a way to gird myself for what was to come.

Cuthbert and I needed some private time so I left for a corner of the barn, out of view, and removed my companion slowly and with care. I knew he was just a piece of wood, but maybe the stress of what was coming led me to speak to my long-time partner, if not in soothing then at least truthful words, to tell him of our predicament and ask him for some self-control.

"Tomorrow and the day after, I'm going to try your patience," I said, looking at Cuthbert while rubbing my stump with Noxzema. "But I have no choice. You'll have every reason to complain, but I'm going to have to ignore you. That's the way it is. Both of us need to be strong." My words were few, part apology, part pep-talk. The truth. It's what I always offered Cuthbert, he being attached to me that way. He always complained when I ignored him and I didn't expect this time would be different. And I don't know if my talk did either of us any good, but being honest felt right. I put on a fresh stump sock and tried to get some rest.

I must have been more tired than I thought. It seemed that just as I lay my head down on the hay and closed my eyes, Miguel opened the barn door, and the cold night air rushed in.

The first words I heard came from the Aussie. "Shit," he said, lifting his head. "It's snowing."

Then came Miguel's demand: "Vamanos." It was going to be a rapid departure. We got up hurriedly and headed to the barn door.

The outside world was one of stark contrast. We were swallowed whole by the dark, a night without a moon or stars, only the bright flakes swirling about us. They reminded me of the butterflies back at Box Horn. Monarchs in the afternoon sun. In the mid-summer months, our fields were home to hundreds of them flitting to and fro without care or worry, traveling in seemingly aimless directions, floating over the terrain with ease. How I envied them now as I entered this cold world of black and white.

It had been snowing for a little while, just an inch or two dusted the ground, and as the trail drifted upward, I tried to ignore the hypnotic effect of the snowflakes rolling toward me.

We stayed in the forest that first hour, but as we climbed higher, the air became thinner, and the majestic trees gave way to smaller mountain pines and, higher still, to scrub brush. The washboard trail became slick, and movements with Cuthbert had to be planned.

Cuthbert's booted foot began to slide more frequently, and as the path turned upward, I took the steeper parts sideways, especially around the larger rocks that now littered the trail. I was glad the Aussie had picked up on Cuthbert, so he understood my frequent awkwardness and need to give boulders a wide birth. The Frenchman and Miguel didn't seem to notice that we were falling farther behind.

As time passed, the snow deepened and the terrain became more uneven, I expected Cuthbert would slip, be pulled rudely from his seat, and come down hard on my stump. Like at Box Horn, when I'd first met Cuthbert and we started walking together. But at the farm, I had parallel bars to catch me and medication to ease the pain. A fall outdoors without support in the snow and ice? I vowed to keep my mouth shut no matter the anguish Cuthbert caused.

My first slip was a small one. Cuthbert gave way and I landed forward; my right hand hit the slick trail and my left landed on a boulder that straddled the path. I pushed off and recovered quickly.

It surprised me how vile I turned after that minor misstep. It happened so unexpectedly, a sign I was losing control, tiring more than I knew. Losing control always is unsettling, and my wooden companion was becoming a pain in the ass. "Pull yourself together, Cuthbert," I said through gritted teeth. A muffled laugh came from behind. I looked around to see the Aussie with a wide grin. "What are you laughing about?" I whispered with annoyance.

"Sorry, but I thought it funny," he said, also in a low voice. "You're blaming your wooden mate for your own misstep. You might consider being a bit more understanding. You know he's a blockhead."

He laughed again, louder this time, but I couldn't find the humor. That blockhead continued taking his revenge every few steps. And over the next hour, I fell again, and I continued swear silently, at Cuthbert, the Aussie, and at myself, too, for being so damn clumsy. Be more understanding. He doesn't have a seven-pound anchor chained to his knee.

That thought became a loop in my mind, and as I began to fix on my condition, my anger grew until it burned white hot. But then something miraculous happened. I became distracted momentarily by a gust of wind and I saw how the individual flakes seemed to move in unison, like a flock of starlings in autumn. That thought carried me again to Box Horn, in fall, with memories of hickory smoke and the maples filled with red and orange leaves. For a moment, I neglected my anger, and when I returned to it, my mind had turned ever so slightly in a way that allowed me to see my condition in a different light. The possibility emerged that just maybe there was something right, a bit of truth behind the Aussie's humor. Many kilometers lay in front of us, and Cuthbert was making me more miserable with each step. Unless something changed, my hate would flare up for all to see.

It was a conscious decision, but I worked to purge my mind of vile thoughts and began to fill it with events from the past: my childhood spent in the forest in Box Horn, climbing into my father's welcoming lap, acting in school plays at the Roland Park School, traveling through old Europe, and of course, those early days with Emil. I made a mental inventory, filed each of these thoughts away much as a squirrel saves acorns for a long winter sleep, and I began to dole them out for consideration, one by one, as the trail became harsher and more demanding.

In recalling a memory, I would try to suck the marrow from each event, remember the detail, the feelings I had, how I'd pleased others or how they had pleased me. It helped that my mind was elsewhere. On the trail, that vile beast, Cuthbert, continued to grind my tender stump. As the pain grew more intense, it became harder to hold my tongue and force my way back to the peaceful terrain of my mind.

Midway through that night, my will lapsed and destructive thoughts encroached again like a relentless enemy sieging a citadel. The most terrifying memories held the faces of those I left behind. They spoke to me, asked me why I abandoned them to be rounded up like cattle for slaughter. The horror of their fate and my responsibility for it dragged me down, and my outlook began to slide. Desperate to find some peace, I made a pledge: I'd return to France. I'd make it right.

My promise offered some temporary comfort but the most vivid images returned during the steepest part of the climb up to the Col de Mantet. The snow, still falling, was two feet deep and the path, perched precariously on the side of the mountain, had narrowed to a two-foot ledge. There was very little to grab onto should I fall, just scrub-brush hidden beneath mounds of snow on the trail's edge. Trudging upward, I forced myself not to look over the dark edge, inches from Cuthbert, and I stabbed my hand into those snow mounds more than once as I slid toward the abyss. There wasn't a patch of my clothing that wasn't covered in white.

The powdery snow was deep, and Cuthbert, unresponsive to my commands, was dragging behind me like a snowplow, blazing a trail of his own. On this intensely harrowing part of the trail, steep and slick, I concentrated on what lay ahead, so the uplifting stories I'd so carefully tended were held in abeyance. But putting them aside left me defenseless against the tidal surge of self-doubt that came rushing in. I tried to stay focused on the trail, but as it became steeper, I used my hands to clamber over icy rocks. My mental outlook turned hideous, and I began to slip with greater frequency. How pitiful I had become.

Look at me now, dragging this piece of wood up and down this goddam mountain. I'm an old, broken-down woman, not strong enough for this challenge. What was I trying to prove? I wasn't good enough for State, for Emil, or any other man. Miguel was right: there's no mercy up here on this cold mountain. I should have stayed in France to die with my agents.

Self-doubt and self-loathing. So unusual for me. Sliding into the black pit of despair, I had no will, no strength to pull myself out. I thought death would provide relief.

But in the recesses of my mind came a faint recollection of another time I'd felt this same way. The memory grew larger. It was my year at Box Horn. How angry I was at myself and the world. How I thrashed about. The hateful things I said to those who cared for me the most.

Then deeper I went, to another remembrance of someone who cared. Of Mother. And her words returned to me: how she spoke of another challenge of my life, my wound in Gediz and how it affected me. How it caused me to think of myself as not good enough, as something less than whole, something less than a complete woman. The memory of my dear mother. Still at home waiting for me. Her words came to me in my misery. I couldn't stop my eyes from filling.

Mother. How hard she'd worked and persevered on the farm after father passed, how much she cared for me. The letters she wrote without expectation of any in return. Her kindness and hopefulness that I would come home safely. I couldn't let her down. I couldn't die here in the ice and snow on this cold mountain. Then as I wiped away new tears, more of her words came to me. She was right. I wasn't brought up to be an angry, bitter woman. Trekking the Pyrenees had become the greatest challenge I'd ever faced. But I'd conquered others in my life, and that gave me the strength to believe. I could overcome this, too.

CHAPTER THIRTEEN

───────

Dindy said the climb over the Pyrenees was the hardest thing she'd
ever done and she was sure the guide would have abandoned her
had he realized she was missing a leg.

Lorna Catling
Virginia Hall's niece

NOVEMBER 1942, MANTET

It was about hour before dawn when we reached the summit
of the Col de Mantet. The snow had stopped, and from the
treeless ridge in the dim light, I could see a clean blanket of
fresh white and smoke rising from chimneys in the small town that
had given the col its name. Miguel and the Frenchman were far
ahead, but their tracks that zigged and zagged down the treeless
slope were clear to follow. Down the mountain and beyond Mantet
was a small river we would ford and farther still, smoke rising from
a cabin.

Seeing our resting place in the distance lifted my spirits, and
despite Cuthbert's appalling behavior, my will, for now, had been
precariously patched. The trail downhill would be demanding, but in
the faint morning light, the slope to the valley floor did not appear as
steep as the path that had led to the col.

Within an hour, we passed through the small town with no more
than ten stone structures close to the banks of the l'Alemany. Cuthbert
was unsteady. I began looking for a narrow, shallow crossing.

"Hey, wait," the Aussie called. He'd found a branch along the
river's bank and broke it to the right size for a staff. "I'll go first to test
the water. In the meantime, use this to steady yourself."

He crossed the frigid, knee-deep, water and I followed, using my
staff to steady myself along the rocky bottom.

I teetered on the rocks but reached the other bank without falling.
A small but satisfying victory. "I only have it half as bad as you," I said,
pointing to Cuthbert.

The Aussie gave a weak smile but didn't laugh. It seemed the cold
and evening's trek had taken a toll on my companion, too. But soon,
we were back on the path trudging upward past a grove of white birch
toward the cabin.

I was never so glad as when I entered the warmth of that hut. The
French partisan had a kettle of simmering porridge hanging over the
fireplace and though he seemed glad to see us, I was in no mood to talk.
One thought was fixed in my mind; the same one that had been with me
for the past four hours. I limped toward a private corner of the one-room
cabin, wrapped a blanket around myself and pulled off my wet clothes,
crusted in snow and ice. Then I unharnessed Cuthbert. Oh, God, it was so
good to be released from all that heavy wet and to have that anchor drop
from my thigh. I began massaging my stump which was sore and red and
didn't give a goddam that Miguel, reclining with his bare feet perched in
front of the fire, had turned his body to watch. It must have been a spectacle
for him. Especially when I winced and pulled Cuthbert off.

"Su puta madre!" Miguel called out.

I'm sure he'd never seen an artificial leg before. His cry drew
everyone's attention, but no one else seemed to care about Cuthbert.
In that moment, I took satisfaction in seeing the shock on his face
wipe away the sneer of contempt. But I didn't waste time on Miguel. I
was tending my stump. The Aussie and Frenchman helped lay my wet
clothes in front of the fire and they began to steam. Water puddled on
the stone hearth.

After getting my fill of porridge, I reclined on a nearby chair. No one talked. Cuthbert, within the tangle of his harness, lay up against the wall. The marks left by the straps that had dug so deeply into the flesh left red and brown bruises that would stay with me for weeks. But I didn't think one whit about events on the mountain or what was to come. For now, I was enjoying the crackle and glow of the fire, happy simply to be. I was exhausted, and it didn't take long for the warmth of the fire to take hold.

I slept soundly that day and my dream, only a snippet, was wonderful and magical. It was a bright spring day, and I was on the ridge of the mountain. Below lay the small stone town of Mantet. Cows were on the mountain slope, their bells clanging as they chewed the early season's tender grass and the townspeople prepared their fields. There was a gentle breeze on my face, which I pointed to the warmth of the sun. How wonderful it would be to soar as high as I could, to view this tranquil scene from the clean, fresh air above. Then miraculously, I sprouted a Monarch's wings and began to fly down the mountain slope to and fro, catching an occasional updraft that pushed me higher still. Soaring without a care or worry in the world.

Butterflies were my favorite creatures especially Monarchs. They endured much—the pain of transformation from an awkward caterpillar to chrysalis to become beings of unmatched beauty and strength, able to fly thousands of miles.

I slept for five hours, as did the others, but our French host woke me a bit early. He had a wireless in the corner and told me that London was on the line, inquiring about my trip. I told him to wire back that I was fine but that Cuthbert was giving me fits. He dutifully tapped the message into his machine, and it wasn't too long afterwards that he returned with a long face. He gave me a response from London. It read:

IF CUTHBERT IS CAUSING PROBLEMS ELIMINATE HIM.

I smiled and told the Frenchman not to worry. My companions were safe.

The evening arrived too soon and while the others were enjoying their first cup of tea, I harnessed Cuthbert into place. It wasn't long before all of us, yawning and stretching, were on our way up the valley. Today would be a long day, and we'd be climbing higher still.

Thankfully, the snow had stopped and the night was clear and still. There was a crunch underfoot, and we started out as we had before, with Miguel racing to the front and the Frenchman close behind. My stump was terribly sore, but for now I was fixed on Miguel's handkerchief wagging in the distance, tossed about by the crisp night breeze.

The Aussie had stayed behind to walk side by side with me. I thought it unusually kind, as he appeared to be the best conditioned of any of us. Still, it was not my way to slow others, and I willingly took charge of my own fate.

"I'm delighted you're still with me," I said, feeling Cuthbert's voracious bite with each step. "But it can't be my scintillating conversation." I turned to my Aussie companion and managed a small smile "You should go ahead.".

"No. I was going to comment on that," he said. "It's something you really need to work on, you know. You're really a dull conversationalist, but I'm content to give you another chance to polish your skills."

We stayed silent for a few moments, just the squeak of cold snow speaking for us.

"I didn't get a chance to thank you properly for paying my way. And now of course," he said with a small twinkle in his eye, "I have the terrible responsibility to see you get home. I couldn't face Miguel if you slipped off the mountain in the night without paying my full fare. Lord knows how he would exact payment."

I was buoyed by the Aussie's comment, but the good feeling was short-lived. As we climbed higher in the dark, I faced a new wave of dread. It was like a horror movie I'd seen in my father's theater for a second time. I'd seen this movie before. And the pain was only part of the battle. The mental challenge—the doubt and all that went with it—again would creep in and wash away my will to push onward.

Pic de la Dona shone like an icy star in the moonlight, and I measured our progress by how close and then how far we had traveled from it. Gratefully, the trail at this point was not steep but it was a relentlessly upward slope. I wasn't sure what was worse, an up-and-down trail or one that continued, even at a gradual rise, relentlessly upward. My mind vacillated on the point. I preferred whatever I wasn't enduring at the time.

As the trail continued to weave higher, a bone-crushing tiredness seemed to grab hold, and the only thought I had in my mind was that I wanted this trek over. But as we traveled farther south across the mountains and through the valleys, the frigid cold seemed to abate, and my spirits lifted when the white gave way to patches of brown and green. The glaciers fed by moist Atlantic air were falling away behind us. Many kilometers remained but as hours slipped by, a drier breeze from the Mediterranean took hold, and temperatures began to rise. The weight on my shoulders pushed Cuthbert more deeply into the mud. I stopped momentarily and was about to abandon my gloves.

"Not so fast," the Aussie said. "It's colder than you think. Wait until we reach the border."

Soon thereafter, Miguel and the Frenchman slowed their advance and crouched behind a shrub. The handkerchief was gone from Miguel's pack, but in the moonlight, the Frenchman waved for us to get low. Then Miguel stood, walked over a ridge, and returned with another man, a guard with a rifle on a leather strap slung low on his shoulder. Miguel walked slowly toward us. The guard stayed behind.

"Carlos says there are four Spanish border guards ahead," Miguel said in a low voice. "And Germans are nearby. Carlos gave me a choice. We take our chances and run across the border, or we wait here for the signal that all's clear." Miguel paused and looked directly into my eyes. "Ten thousand francs—a small price for the signal that gives you freedom. And yes, it frees both of us. Once in Spain, I am free of you, lady-with-a-wooden-leg."

Carlos and Miguel were partners, but I let it pass. I had just trekked the goddam Pyrenees in the snow and ice, dragging Cuthbert behind me. Miguel? He was merely a housefly buzzing about my head.

But before paying, I pressed Miguel for more information. "What's security like beyond the border?"

"Spanish police and, yes, Germans, but they are not in charge. You follow the road down through Setcases to the train at San Juan de las Abadesas."

I pulled out my billfold and gave Miguel five thousand. "You know the agreement. The rest on the other side of the border."

Miguel looked at the money and thumbed through it as he walked to the border guard. He handed Carlos a few bills and stuffed the rest in his shirt.

About a half hour later in the early morning light, we received the signal: a woman across the border hung a bedsheet on a clothesline. Others ran but I dragged Cuthbert through the mud and beyond the rickety barbed wire gate that was the border. Exhausted by the mountain trek across the Pyrenees, we were free. At last.

Just past the border, Miguel stood waiting. I was content to pull out my billfold that last time and stayed silent as I thumbed through the cash. Paying was a milestone: liberation, freedom, and another step closer to home.

As Miguel walked away, I let out a breath that came from deep inside. More miles separated us from the train station at San Juan de las Abadesas, but a great weight had been lifted from our backs. I told myself the worst was over, and that thought pushed me through the sheer exhaustion and pain of dragging Cuthbert those extra miles.

I don't know how we made it through the Spanish villages of Compradon, Setcases and, finally, San Juan de Las Abadesas. It was all a blur. But the thought of freedom and what I'd overcome helped distract me from Cuthbert's ravenous appetite.

Our arrival at the train station must have been quite a scene that early morning. Me, dirty, salt stains across my forehead and eyes, in clothes I had been wearing for three days, dragging a prosthetic limb behind me. My companions looked weary and exhausted too. I gave a nod to my Aussie friend and the Frenchman farther down the platform, and I lipped the words thank you. The Aussie gave a weak smile in return, and now I was waiting for the train totally unaware of my foolish, unconscionable mistake.

We arrived at the train station at 4:30 a.m. for a train leaving at 5:45, thinking it was all over. The end to my pain had come. After all those miles walking, now I was on the verge of *being conveyed* to my destination. The consulate in Barcelona was in sight. I could see it. Feel it. Luxuriate in the thought of tending to my needs: separated from Cuthbert in a bath, soothing my blistered wound; a glass of Spanish red in my hand on a warm veranda overlooking the Mediterranean, eating real food.

I could blame it on exhaustion and weariness. But really, it was an appalling lack of commonsense. All of it led me to let my guard down. In my haste to leave Lyon I hadn't forged an *entrada* stamp for my passport. So when the border guards asked to see my papers, it was clear I'd entered illegally. Spanish jail. Figueras. Goddammit.

CHAPTER FOURTEEN

I've given this a good four months try and came to the conclusion that (being in Spain) really is a waste of time and money. Anyhow, I always did want to go back to France. When I came out here I thought I'd be able to help F Section people but I don't and can't. I'm not doing a job. I'm simply living pleasantly and wasting time. It isn't worthwhile and after all, my neck is my own, and . . . I'm willing to get a crick in it because there's a war . . .

VIRGINIA HALL LETTER TO MAURICE BUCKMASTER
ABOUT SEPTEMBER 1943

It is only because I honestly believe that the gestapo would also know (of your return) in about a fortnight that I say no . . . You are really too well-known in the country and it would be wishful thinking believing you could escape . . . we do not want to give (Klaus Barbie) even half a chance by sending in anyone as remarkable as yourself.

MAURICE BUCKMASTER'S REPLY LETTER
6 OCTOBER 1943

DECEMBER 1942, FIGUERAS PRISON, SPAIN

I had committed a cardinal sin of espionage. Really, it's basic spy tradecraft drilled into all SOE agents in Group B training. Look and listen. Assess your surroundings. Perform a surveillance detection route. Pass your destination several times. And one more rule: never, ever, arrive early to an appointment.

I'm convinced that if my mind hadn't been so addled by the three-day trek, I'd never have stumbled onto the platform over an hour early for the Barcelona train. I knew my passport was incomplete, no *entrada* stamp, but I was in a hurry to leave Lyon, and then once we arrived, Cuthbert's need for rest overruled my basic instincts. Maybe I had been too exhausted to care.

I had time to think about it in the stone fortress in Figueras, the Castelle de Sant Ferran. It had a luxurious sounding name, but it was as filthy as all the rest. The dark and damp communal cells—a dungeon complete with cold granite walls and rock-hard bunks—the prison was filled with a strange mix of inmates: Spanish nationals on the wrong side of Franco, desperate people like me who had crossed the border illegally, murderers, petty thieves, and all the other undesirables Spain could jam into that disgraceful building circled by barbed wire. It wasn't a place of physical brutality like Fresnes or Beyelmy. The brutality I suffered was self-imposed. I flogged myself mercilessly. When would I be set free? I had no idea.

Not being patient was a character flaw, but during my painful escape over the mountains, I'd fantasized about Barcelona. Away from all the cold and snow, recuperating on a sunny rooftop balcony above the sea, and I'd imagined that when Cuthbert ceased to be annoying, I'd work my way back into Buck's France Section of SOE. Now my dreams had been delayed, and I was rotting away on a filthy bunk waiting for someone to realize I was missing.

My anxiety was doubled because I'd collected intelligence on Vichy, rumors that former Minister of Defense, Maxime Weygand, had been arrested and Philippe Petain, Head of State, might resist the Germans now that they'd invaded Free France. Good intelligence

London needed. I'd carried all of it on scraps of paper across the Pyrenees and drafted a coded letter for London. The propagandists would use it—in newspapers and on the radio—to rally the French. But I hadn't yet found a way to smuggle the letter to the British consulate, much less tell them I was in prison.

So there I was, covered in grime, stuck in the filth, marking time watching the vermin skitter across the concrete floor, with an important message for London burning a hole in my pocket. Cleanliness was impossible. Three hundred inmates on my floor were served by a single water tap. And the slop they fed me was the kind of regurgitated mash I remember feeding the swine at Box Horn.

I figured two, three days at most before the consulate would rescue me. If I were destined for a long stay I'd have considered a jail break. But as the wasted days piled up my irritation burned more brightly, and after three weeks with no one from the consulate in sight, I began reconsidering my options. One of my cellmates, a tart convicted of turning tricks but not making the police payoff, was about to be set free. Would she be so kind as to give the British consulate a letter for my cousin Nic?

My coded message to SOE included a personal note: Goddammit! Get me the hell out of Figueras. Now!

Two days later the Brits had officials from the American consulate come to collect their wayward agent, and together we walked through the heavy wrought iron gate. My penalty? The Spanish gave me three months' probation and extracted a promise not to do it again.

I was hugely relieved finally to be out of that rats' nest. My anger cooled, and what annoyance remained was directed at Cuthbert for his hateful behavior over the Pyrenees. But by then, I was gaining some time and distance from my ghastly trek.

*   *   *

SOE wanted a debriefing on my fifteen months in the Haute Loire, so after a few days of divine renovation in a warm bathtub, Cuthbert and I caught a flight to London. They wanted the debriefing, and they would get it. But I'd also use the time to get something I wanted.

Prison had given me time to think about my next move: how to make good on my promise made in the mountains. Was it too late for my agents? I'd try to find that out, but there was more work to be done liberating France. I had left something of myself in the Haute Loire and had to go back to reclaim it. Someone who didn't know me might have called it bravado but I called it being realistic. No one else had my skills and field experience. Already, I'd set my mind on my return.

It was the week of Christmas, and back in London, Buck invited me to lunch in SOE's executive dining room on Baker Street. I was met at the entrance by Park, dressed in a black butler jacket, who welcomed me back, calling me 3844. With a nod and a little gesture, he motioned to the back room.

The room held only a few tables and was a place of starched linens and black waiters in white jackets standing against the wall. But today, the only decoration was a single sad strand of red garland drooping from the corners of the high ceiling. Everyone was so busy with the war. But there Buck was, alone, seated and staring intently at his menu.

Buck looked up and broke into a broad smile. As he rose from his chair, he made a show of throwing his linen napkin onto the spotless tablecloth. He greeted me with an extended hand, then pulled me close for a shoulder hug.

"Bloody good to see you, Dindy," Buck said still holding me. "If I had known in advance, I would have had our consulate send a car to pick you up at the border. None of this prison business." He shook me once then released me. "But you came out in the dead of the night. We had no idea where you were and then, of course, it was too late. But," he said, looking me in the eye and wagging his finger, "I never doubted for a minute that you'd make it out. You are quite a formidable woman, you know."

"Well," I said, rolling over his compliment, "what's done is done. There are things I'd have done differently, but I'll save all that for the debriefing."

"Brilliant," Buck said, sitting down, unfurling his napkin and sliding it from the table to his lap. His sharp retort told me this wasn't the time to talk about Alesh, Le Chatte, or the trail of breadcrumbs that led to Heckler. All would be revealed in time.

The debriefing would be done by London SOE counterespionage. I'd seen the CE-types before, those thin-lipped, pale-skinned trolls who would lead me to a windowless room to discuss the details of betrayal and list what was lost. It wouldn't be pleasant. Interviews with counterespionage never were. They were a different breed. It was CE's job to peer at you with their small black eyes, scrutinize your moves, use sharp tones to uncover rocks, and make you admit to some triviality of poor tradecraft. But their endless questions, many the same but asked slightly differently, *were so tiresome*. They didn't trust anyone—except themselves, of course. Their starting point was that I was responsible for Heckler's demise. And it was true, trusting others but not my own instincts. I shared the guilt. An accusation I couldn't deny.

Buck and I understood each other's lunchtime agenda. There would be time to reconnect with pleasantries, remember times past, talk a bit about Vera and people we knew in common, laugh where we could, and speak in somber tones of those who didn't make it back, but it was up to me to push the central question: What's next?

I imagined that Buck would dance around the subject, not wanting to commit to anything, while I'd seek clarity. I'd use logic, stay cool, tell him I was the most experienced damn agent he had in France. But I wouldn't overplay my hand. He'd want me in the cooler, out of the business for some indefinite period. And when I returned, it wouldn't be to France. No one burned could ever return.

Buck wouldn't understand my need to go back. I'd committed so much of myself to the field, took on new personalities, and fashioned my identities so completely that they could only live in that niche of the world. I couldn't give them up, not when there was real work to be done. They were my creation, part of me. Even more, I suppose, than Cuthbert.

But it was the danger that gave my characters life. Recruiting spies. Meeting in forbidden locations. Collecting secrets under the noses of those who would kill you. That was what made the blood pulse through my veins, heightened my senses, made me see the world with a clarity few outside of it could comprehend. And then there were my agents. Guerin, Rousset, and all the others I had abandoned. That stain could only be removed by my return. And here I was, in London, only a few dozen miles from the fight. I couldn't stand not being back in France. I wouldn't be sidetracked.

In the choreography of our lunch, I'd agree to stay put for a short while, work behind the scenes, but my return to France was non-negotiable. All of us knew that the façade of invincible Germany was crumbling, but before things went to hell on the continent, I'd find my agents and be part of Europe's liberation.

"You know, Buck," I said. "I've been thinking. We haven't scratched the surface using the maquis. We need to bring the Communists, Catholics, and Gaullist Resistance together for joint sabotage operations. Now, I know they aren't a natural fit, but if London gave us that goddam green light, I'd get things started. Develop the cadre of fighters ready for D-Day. Then we'd attack. . ." I stopped midsentence.

My speech had started calmly enough, but it had grown louder and more strident. Too passionate for a first lunchtime meeting.

Buck looked away and stayed silent, content to let me talk myself out.

I didn't apologize. "I seem to be getting ahead of myself. I've thought this through and have plans for the field."

Buck hesitated. "Yes. Yes. Ahemm," he said, clearing his throat, "the field." He reached for a glass of water. "Since you raised it," he said between sips, "let's talk about you, shall we?" He put the glass down. "You know the CE-types have a million questions about your time in Lyon, so you'll stay put here in London for a while."

"Yes. But my follow-on?"

"After your debrief? Well, that will take some time. But yes, your follow-on assignment." Buck was fidgeting with his starched napkin. He pulled it from his lap and laid it on the table. "It's not fully settled, of course, but the chief, Gubbins, wants you back in Spain working with the escape and evasion people. Gubbins says—and I agree—that we need to do a better job planning escapes from France and keeping track of agents coming over the mountains," Buck said, appearing to be mildly embarrassed. "You've seen firsthand and what a mess we've made of it with your journey, and we'll put your experience to work. And now that the Germans are extending the *zone interdit* to the mountains, well, it's a sticky wicket, indeed."

My eyes were elsewhere, and I was fidgeting with my napkin.

But he continued anyway. "We need good recruitments, Spanish agents who can help get our people over the hump and out of jail. It won't be easy. With Franco cozying up to Jerry, Spain's neutrality is just a technicality. The government is swaying with the breeze, open to the highest bidder, so the place is a nest of spies. The Nazis are working to undermine us in Spain just as they are in France and the rest of the continent . . . Dindy? Dindy! Did you hear anything I said?"

In truth, I'd fixed on one word. "Spain?"

"Now, I know you want to jump back into the thicket. But France is too hot. Gubbins says definitely not. It's off-limits. Barbie has your face on wanted posters all over France. He put a price on your head. Called you the most dangerous spy, for Christ's sake. Surely you can't . . ." Buck had that furrowed brow. It was the look he gave when he was backed into a corner and knew he had a fight on his hands.

He paused, then chose a different tack. "Look, France is now a different place than when you were there. It's much more dangerous and brutal now that the Germans have taken over the whole country. Summary executions, grisly torture. Our agents are being sent off with the Jews to suffer and die horribly in the camps." His voice undulated, and he wagged his head slightly from side to side. "I can tell you, France is no place for a woman."

Buck must have seen the fire in my eyes. He shifted in his seat and looked away uncomfortably. "Vera wouldn't have been happy with that comment, and now that I've said it, neither am I," he said sheepishly. "Well, what I really meant is that SOE, we, we can't be callous and indifferent to your safety. Knowing what I do about the situation, and knowing how badly the gestapo wants you, I couldn't forgive myself if I sent you in now. It would be a suicide mission."

I made no effort to hide the annoyance still on my face. "Buck, you and I both know I'm the best goddam agent F Section has. Does Gubbins realize what he's losing by dumping me in Spain? It's my neck, and if I want to get a crick in it, it's my right. Tell *that* to Gubbins."

Buck looked exasperated and gave it another try, this time softening his voice. "Look here, Dindy, you've done great things, but I'm responsible for you, for other SOE agents, and for the entire F Section enterprise. It's not just your skin. If—no, *when*—you're discovered, you'll endanger not just yourself but the other agents working with you, and I just can't have that on my conscience. Now, you and that Cuthbert of yours have shown yourself adept at escaping the Jerrys. SOE needs your talents, and Spain is where we need you most."

Dammit. Buck wasn't going to push my case with Gubbins. At least not yet.

"And if something opens up?" I asked.

"You're still a France Section agent, just working for the escape-and-evasion people for a while. Dindy, take the job. For now, take Spain."

OCTOBER 1943, MADRID

My debriefing in London was an exhausting and drawn-out affair that lasted through the spring of 1943. Counterespionage wanted everything I had on the double agents Alesh and Le Chatte and others who might be involved in deceit. They wanted to know what I knew about the roll-up of France Section circuits, names and addresses of reliable French assets, and where in Haute Loire the resistance was strongest and weakest.

I answered each of these and many more questions with as much patience as I could muster, though I was close to losing it all more than once when they switched interviewers but continued hammering the same questions. It seemed no one was listening. I ended each session with questions of my own: What do you know about my agents back in the Haute Loire—Madame Guerin, Doctor Rousset, Suzanne Bertillon, the Labouriers, Madame Catin?

But each of my questions was met with icy silence. They didn't answer questions, they just asked them. It gave me the worst feeling imaginable—anxiety spawned by helplessness mixed with feelings of responsibility.

I supposed that if I had to be on ice before heading to Spain, London was a better place than most. At least I'd be near the action. Since I had left France, the Germans had taken off the gloves, and so had the Allies. Activity was at a fevered pace: SOE agents coming in and departing; new circuits forming across France; Lizzys loaded with high explosives, guns and ammunition making drops in the French countryside; the maquis being organized in different regions; and most important, the beginning of organized sabotage operations. My heart was racing, so close to being there. Just twenty miles and I'd be taking the war to the Germans too.

Along the way, I ran into an old friend, Bill Grell, manager of the St. Regis in New York, who now was in London with the Office of Strategic Services, the new American espionage organization and counterpart to Britain's SOE. Grell, an agreeable sort, had the open face of a Labrador Retriever and was just as willing to lavish his attention on me without reservation. As one of America's first OSS officers to work directly with SOE, Bill delighted in telling me about his training regime with his British counterparts, learning spy trade-craft, wireless communications, weapons, explosives and all the rest.

He said OSS and SOE would work together in France prior to D-Day, but he didn't yet know how it would all fit together. At the time, he had no idea I was working for SOE. I'd promised not to reveal my SOE employment with anyone, including the Americans. But I didn't know what the future held, and Grell seemed the right kind of American officer to cultivate.

*   *   *

The news coming from the continent was turning favorable with conditions ripening for an all-out assault on the continent. The

Germans were out of North Africa. To the east, the Russians had forced the Nazis to retreat from a bloody siege at Stalingrad. And in September, Italy succumbed to Allied assaults and surrendered. All around, the German empire was crumpling, but their hold on central Europe—and all of France—was a desperate death grip and with it came a willingness to commit any atrocity imaginable to maintain power.

In London, I received personal letters that SOE had been holding. There was a backlog from Mother, who had written every week, and I read each one. But after the fifth or sixth, their content, well, I'd heard it all before: the rabbits got into the garden again; Matilde the cow wouldn't produce; the cute new lamb was born black. Mother must have sensed the sameness, too, and began peppering her letters with talk of politics and baseball.

When I started writing again in London, my letters weren't any better than hers. They were short and vague, the minimum really. Not because I didn't want to reciprocate, but there was so very little I was allowed to say. Whether she smiled on opening the mailbox, I'll never know, but I imagined she did, and merely by affixing postage, I was laying to rest her worst fears.

It occurred to me that beyond the ordinary prose of our letters, there was a secondary meaning buried deep between the lines, like the coded messages I had written to London. The letters and words meant little. The implicit meaning of Mother's letters was unwavering, always simple, clear, direct. We didn't say it very often—that that wasn't the Hall family way. Love was the coded content unmistakably etched within each of Mother's letters. Our mutual affection had grown stronger over the years, and we both knew it would endure regardless of what happened on the farm at Box Horn or on the battlefield in France.

Mother knew how strongly I felt about being in this fight, and I suppose she knew, too, her responsibility for the turn I had taken toward this life of espionage. Maybe she regretted that part of it. The danger. But that was the risk she had taken when she grasped my shoulders and shook me from my depression, when she made me think beyond Gediz and pointed the way. The rest of it had been up to me. And then I found my second chance at life in France. And the deeper I'd been drawn into the complex web of espionage, the more confident I had become. Along the way, I'd changed and become the character I was playing. Now away from France and what I was meant to do, I'd become lost. Going back was the only thing that made sense. No one could convince me otherwise.

*   *   *

Rain in Madrid. The weather that day of my arrival in mid-May only served to deepen my already sour mood. I was told that for the first eight weeks, I was to reestablish my credentials as a *New York Post* correspondent for the benefit of the Spanish authorities. But almost immediately my cover developed complications. George Backer in New York sent a telegram saying there wasn't enough reader interest to support a Madrid correspondent. It was his way of telling me my cover wouldn't be credible, it wouldn't hold, if I stayed in Spain. So, I'd have to find a new employer to vouch for me. I couldn't blame the *Post*. It was right and its decision not to offer cover confirmed what I already knew. Spain was a sideshow in the war, and now I was merely a spectator on the sidelines watching the world go by. But I landed quickly on my feet. The *Chicago Times* agreed to sponsor me.

Abetting escapes over the Pyrenees was mostly a sit-down job, much too tame for my tastes. I organized exits, tracked who was coming over the mountains, and arranged safe houses along the way. Part of the time I recruited Spaniards, took them out for a meal, plied them with alcohol, put money in their pocket and kept paying them as long as they kept our people out of jail. I repeated the process again and again. Some might have thought this a plum assignment. No real danger. Comfortable surroundings. Eating and drinking from an expense account. I was thoroughly bored.

SOE tied me up with trivial tasks—trips to the border to pick up agents, then drop them off at the consulate. Back to the border. Then the consulate. It was so excruciating that, I admit, in my spare time, I nibbled at the edges of insubordination. Buck must have known I wouldn't be tied down, and I didn't care. My family of agents might have been holding on in Haute Loire or on the run or being chased by the gestapo or worse. They still needed me, and here I was twiddling my thumbs. But how could I regain contact? Then it came to me. Christine 25.

Though I didn't know where she was, trying to contact Christine was strictly forbidden, outside my area of responsibility. I'm sure some would have called it freelancing, but I was willing to take the risk. I made contact with Madame Cirera, who organized Christine's chain of couriers over the Pyrenees. But only frustration came of it. Cirera told me France was so chaotic it was impossible and too dangerous to find Christine or contact any of my agents. Another avenue closed.

*   *   *

It was July, two months into my new assignment in Madrid, and I was feeling low when a cable arrived from London:

```
Inform virginia she has been awarded the mbe,
repeat, mbe stop congratulate her on behalf of
buckmaster, boddington, morel and all members
of soe stop in view of her nationality and
cover essential celebrations must remain
strictly private end.
```

Member of the British Empire. It was a great honor. I thanked my superiors and said I was most grateful.

But really, my first thought was, *How can I keep this quiet?* Unless I tamped it down, the publicity surrounding that blasted medal would spread like a wildfire in the August grass. Blow my cover. I'd become damaged goods, and my career in espionage would be over. My second thought? Honestly, I thought it was the gold watch you receive at retirement. The capstone of a career. The pat on the head for a job well done. Sure, I had done some good work, but the award made me suspicious that SOE had cast me aside and had no plans to send me back to France. I was disconsolate. The door was slamming shut, and I wouldn't be part of France's liberation after all.

I declined meeting the king, saying it was for security reasons.

I never did pick up the MBE citation.

I'd just as soon have forgotten the whole thing.

I was miserable sitting on the bench in Spain while the rest of the team was in the field doing the real work. So in October, the time had come for me to force the truth, to push back against the bureaucracy and have them show their hand.

I laid it out for Buck in a letter. Told him I had given it four months, but I was twiddling my thumbs in Spain, wasting time and money. Besides, Leon the Aussie and Jean the Frenchman, who had crossed the Pyrenees with me, had asked me to return to France with them to assist, after training, as their wireless operator. Would London train me for wireless work? It was a good story. Before the war, I'd been a code clerk, still knew morse, and besides, SOE always was short wireless operators, and this was a way to help. A way back into France.

Buck's response came quickly. I suppose he was only reflecting what Gubbins was saying, but the answer, still, was no. I was too well known. Barbie was still hunting me. I'd be captured. He threw up all kinds of blather. Seemed there was no arguing with him. Still, to his credit, he sensed how miserable I was in Spain, and I suppose I should have been grateful that in closing, he threw me a bone.

```
There's a job opening up, briefing the boys,
and when officers from here go into the
field around D-Day, you will be in the right
place. I obviously can make no promises, but
it is a possibility.
```

A briefing officer. It would be another sit-down job away from the field, not a perfect match, but I'd be doing some real work back in London, where I'd have room to maneuver. And the way I was bitching about being bored, well, my supervisors in Spain were delighted to get rid of me.

JANUARY 1944, LONDON

I had made it a habit to push my bounds, exceed expectations. For my first mission, Geologist-5, Buck had said, "Keep your ears and eyes open and report back." Before long I was recruiting and running agents, and Heckler had been central to SOE operations in France. A three-month mission had extended to fifteen. Buck had always underestimated me, and that didn't change after returning from Madrid. Since I was receiving uncertain signals about a return to France, it made me think I needed a Plan B. I never doubted I was going back, even if he did.

I kept my vow not to reveal my SOE employment to my American colleagues, but even before taking the job in Spain, I asked Grell to introduce me to his supervisor. Could the Office of Strategic Services gainfully employ the talents of a news correspondent who had spent the last fifteen months behind the lines in Vichy and spoke French, German, Russian, Italian, and Spanish?

Now back in London, I met Bill for lunch and congratulated him on his new assignment: heading up the OSS supply operations in France. Then I told him, in an off-handed way, that we might be colleagues. My interviews progressed, and later that afternoon I had an appointment with David Bruce. A fellow native of Baltimore, Bruce no longer was with the Red Cross. Now he was head of the European Theater of Operations for the OSS.

I wanted Buck to hear it straight from me; I owed him that much. He wasn't happy with my stirring the pot, meeting with Bruce that way. But dammit, he should have known how important it was to me. My return to France. It was all I'd thought about and talked about for the past fourteen months. What did he expect me to do after running into the stone wall with Gubbins? Still, meeting Bruce could poison the well. But the way I saw it, I had nothing to lose.

My message to Bruce was simple. I was fully trained, knew the terrain, the enemy, and all SOE agents in the field. Could anyone do a better job helping the Brits and Americans work together in the France?

The only objection he raised was the circumstances of my escape. Was I burned irreparably? Would I endanger myself and others if I returned?

Nothing of the sort. I told him what I had told Buck earlier, downplaying the danger—that I hadn't really been burned, because the gestapo didn't have enough to go on to capture me—only my pseudonym, the description of a woman with a limp, and an old address with a blown circuit. I could go back into France in disguise with a new name and phony documents, and be up and running on day one. I was fully aware of the dangers and chose to accept them.

Bruce was all business, silent, and took all of it in.

I didn't challenge him. Put all of it on the table in a composed way. My final words came out a bit thick but they were true—as true as anything I'd said before: "I'm an American citizen, and I believe in this cause. We have to win this war, and I simply must help the Allies retake France."

Bruce listened, stroked his narrow chin a few times but didn't reveal himself. At the end, he gave a small nod, thanked me, and said he needed to talk it over with his British colleague, Gubbins, and General Donovan, Head of the OSS. Bruce would get back to me within 48 hours.

I had gone into that meeting full of confidence, thinking it would be an easy sell, but coming out, I wasn't so sure. Goddam Gubbins. A wild card and my greatest antagonist. If he poisoned the well, OSS might not take me and I'd never make it back to France.

Those next two days were hell. I stayed sequestered, out of touch with Americans and British colleagues, holed up in Claridge's near Grosvenor Square, pacing and vacillating minute to minute on my prospects. Was it all sewn up or all lost? I honestly couldn't tell.

Exactly forty-eight hours after my meeting, the phone rang. It was Bruce: "The boss, General Donovan, wants to see you tomorrow at O-nine hundred."

CHAPTER FIFTEEN

The OSS didn't want to send (Virginia Hall) back to France either. She was too well known—but she was quite insistent. If she learned radio, she could serve usefully. They dropped her into France at the time of the invasion.

WILLIAM CASEY
CHIEF, SECRET INTELLIGENCE, OSS
DIRECTOR, CIA 1981-1987

JANUARY 1944, LONDON

The OSS director's office was a vast space with tall windows, thick dentil molding, and heavy red velvet curtains. General Donovan was seated ramrod straight in a rolling, leather high-back chair. He waved me in and pointed to a brown chair with gold tacks opposite his oak desk. The director's secretary, dressed stylishly in a yellow and pink pastel print and a thin hat tilted to one side, closed the thick oak door behind me.

"Sit down, Hall. Sit down." Donovan's voice was hard, but when he spoke my name, it echoed softly off the walls. He stayed focused on a neat ream at the center his otherwise clean desk.

"Just got off the phone with Gubbins," the director said, lifting his penetrating blue eyes from the stack. He tucked his stocky hands behind his head of slicked-back gray-white hair, and the springs in his chair squeaked as he leaned back. "You're in rare company, Hall.

Seems the gestapo has a name for you," he said, slowing his speech. "Barbie calls you *Artemis*. The goddam Greek goddess of the hunt. The queen of the animal kingdom and the wilderness. His perverse sense of humor, I suppose."

I straightened my blue linen skirt and leaned forward. I should have been frightened by being singled out by the gestapo chief, that butcher Klaus Barbie, but I rather liked the name he had given me. Artemis. Perhaps he knew me better than I thought.

"The point is you're still a target, a prize they want to track, kill and stuff into their corner curio. Gubbins says the wanted posters are still up. Informers are waiting to crawl out of the woodwork to collect the bounty. Gubbins is dead set against you going back to France."

Goddam Gubbins. As I sat there across from Donovan, all seemed lost. But I rallied and put aside the thought of defeat. I'd make one last push. It was almost on my lips—it would be a horrible waste to keep a trained agent twiddling her thumbs in London when there was real work in France—but I kept my mouth shut. Maybe Donovan hadn't made up his mind and wanted to talk through his argument. I'd see which way the general was bending before speaking up.

"I'm in a bind," he said. "D-Day's coming, and I don't have any goddam people on the ground." He gave a quick push, and the chair squeaked again as he rose to walk the red Oriental runner with a path worn. "Three OSS officers in France—that's all I've got—and they're working SOE circuits. That asshole Gubbins," he said, his thick jaw tightening, "he has his foot on the gas. Over the last few months, he's doubled the number of agents in the field, while I've got my thumb stuck up my ass." He stopped and looked at me. "For Christ's sake, the war will be over before we jump in. It's time we took off our goddam training wheels."

Donovan walked past me with his hands clenched tightly behind his back. He pivoted as if in a parade, but his gaze stayed on the floor. "Just before D-Day, the Resistance will come down from the hills like ants at a picnic to soften-up German defenses. OSS already would have trained them in automatic weapons and plastic explosives. But before we can parachute in, we need more landing zones, safe houses, and wireless operators."

He paused. My face flushed, and my heart was pounding. Donovan looked up.

"That's where you come in," he said.

"Am I . . . ?"

"You're going back to France."

A broad grin swept across my face. So it was true. I tried to focus on what followed but was lost in my own thoughts. What I'd waited for, dreamed about, was going to happen. I was going back after all. To France.

Donovan, now standing behind his desk, began to tell me how the continent had changed since I was there in '42. That the German's world was collapsing—Italy, North Africa, the Russian Front—and with D-Day coming, the Nazis would do anything, commit any atrocity, some inconceivable in their cruelty, to keep their stranglehold on the country. I suppose he was giving me one last chance to say no.

"They tell me you don't scare easy," he said, "so I'll give it to you straight. Your chances of surviving another round in France are about even . . . well, less than even if you take that radio job." He walked slowly past my chair again and sat on the edge of his desk, so close I could smell his musk aftershave. "The German direction-finding vans and planes are good. Damn good. You hear about Cartigny? Gubbins says they found him slumped over his radio. His brains were blown out but his headset was still on."

He lowered his voice, considering his comment. "Poor bastard. Well, I suppose worse things can happen. If Barbie finds you," Donovan said, "well, you know all of that already. You'll carry an L-tab, of course."

I harbored no romantic notions about my return, but Donovan's casual mention of that lima bean-sized pill, that lethal dose of cyanide used when the worst seemed imminent, brought me back to my Class B training. Crush the tablet between your teeth and inhale the vapors I was told, and within fifteen seconds the pill would execute its black magic. The instructor said it was painless. But then how would he know?

"I hear you're made of stout stuff," said Donovan. "If I can't wave you off from going back, Bruce is next door. He'll fill you in on the details." As the director stood up, his secretary in the print dress appeared from nowhere, and the last thing I heard was the door's heavy latch clicking slowly behind me.

I was escorted across the anteroom, past a desk stacked with neat piles of paper and a typewriter, to a door directly facing the director's. The secretary gave two quick knocks and entered without waiting for a response.

David Bruce, the head of European Theater Operations for OSS, was standing next to his desk. "Good to see you, Hall," the colonel said.

Now that we were on the same team, Bruce was less formal than the last time I'd been in his office. With a long thin face and a voice like silk, he recalled how impressed he was on first meeting me. January 1941 seemed so long ago. I'd just arrived in London, fresh from the front, an ambulance driver with the French 9th Ambulance Service Division in Paris. He'd remembered my briefing to embassy staff on my escape that summer of 1940. But he cut the remembrance short. We had more pressing concerns. My upcoming mission.

"I don't know how much the boss told you," Bruce said, motioning to the Chippendale sofa. "You won't be going in by parachute—no need to tuck that wooden leg of yours under your arm. At the end of March, during the new moon, the Brits will take you by torpedo boat to the coast of Brittany, what the French call the Nez Rouge. Until then, you'll finish wireless training at Special Training Site 52, then you'll be off. You'll be going in with a partner codenamed Aramis. He's your team leader for our first circuit. Saint. The main force of OSS will come in soon after you land, to help prepare the maquis for D-Day sabotage operations, whenever that rolls around."

Bruce stood up. "Your mission with Aramis is to find three safe houses around Paris, set up communications, and establish landing zones for our Lysanders and de Havillands farther south." He turned silent.

"And then?" I asked.

"You'll wait in the safe houses and offer support to whoever arrives by land or air."

Something was missing. Maybe I hadn't heard all of what the colonel had to say. "Three safe houses and a few landing zones," I said, more as a question than a statement.

"You might think it a small mission, Virginia, but Paris is the prize. A magnet for German and Allied attention. And once the fighting starts . . ." the colonel stopped mid-thought. "Well, setting up a communications post, reporting back, all while dodging the gestapo will be more difficult than you might think."

The bile was beginning to burn the back of my throat. I'd been dodging the gestapo for months, and this minor, almost inconsequential mission was a mismatch for my background. Christ, I had recruited spies and organized Heckler. Now I'm second fiddle with a mission to set up, and then babysit a few safe houses and landing zones? OSS was being far too cautious. I was about to tell Bruce so, but before I spoke a word, I remembered my instructions for my first mission in France.

Back in '41, Buck had said, "Be our eyes and ears in France and report back." That was before I turned Heckler into a center of espionage: recruiting spies, organizing jail breaks, supporting agents in the field. Dammit! People had been underestimating me from the beginning, and they were still doing it. Why did they have low expectations? Was it for some protective, paternalistic reason? There were so few women with command authority in the field.

I wasn't one to overanalyze a situation, but did find it curious that I seemed to be placed in positions where people expected little of me. And this mission, like the others, seemed to fit a pattern. Maybe I work best when expectations are low and no one is looking over my shoulder. Before Buck and the rest of SOE realized it, I'd become indispensable to the old boys. This Saint business, coming up with a few safe houses wouldn't take long. An organizer with a bit of backbone and a wireless could go anywhere, and maybe I'd move beyond Paris, back to the Haute Loire. But it could be sticky, I did have a partner.

I was thinking of the possibilities, my hand on the doorknob, when Bruce grabbed my elbow.

"Oh yes, one last thing," he said. "This man who will be traveling with—your team lead, Aramis. He's an okay sort. He'll blend in. The Germans will never suspect he's one of ours."

I turned toward Bruce, who wore an odd half-smile. There was more to the story. I faced him directly and let the silence sink in.

"Let's just say your new partner, Aramis, he's 62, our *most senior* agent. Experienced, you might say. And both of you, you're going in as a team, an elderly couple. Aramis and Diane. Now, we'll need to do something about your appearance," Bruce said scrutinizing my face. "Being known to the gestapo and all. The boss did tell you to take the surgery . . ."

My jaw slackened. Had I heard him right? Surgery. *Surgery to rearrange my face?* First startled, then appalled, I calmed myself. No. I'd had more than enough surgery in Turkey, thank you. I'd do damned near anything for my new role. I'd prepare for reentering France as I would for any important theatrical performance: makeup, dress, even working on my posture and gait to play the role of Aramis's elderly partner. But cut up my face to appear old?

Bruce must have noticed my look of bewilderment. He didn't ask again.

My two months at STS 52, on the outskirts of London, passed quickly. I wasn't the fastest or most accurate pianist, but I acquitted myself quite well with the dots and dashes of Morse code—recalled from my code clerk days in the War Department—and I immersed myself in the details of cyphers, codes, and encryption techniques. Though a good student, I was chided more than once by my instructor when I skipped class to attend the cinema in London. Cuthbert and I could only take so much of that stuffy classroom. And those hard chairs. Unrelenting.

When the day of our final examination arrived, I was given a map of London and a twenty-five-pound suitcase with my wireless. I trudged all around town, from building to building. At each stop on my clandestine tour, I found a secret location, set up my machine, unfurled the seven-foot wire antenna, and transmitted a series of messages on assigned frequencies. On departing, I'd add a wig or a scarf or wire-rimmed glasses to alter my appearance. Then off to the next stop, repeating my steps. All the while, security, with their own direction-finding apparatus, searched for me. As hard as they looked, I was never found.

MARCH 1944, PORTSMOUTH, ENGLAND

It was an ungodly hour, two a.m., that day in late March when I arrived at the dock with two battered suitcases in hand. The one that wasn't filled with wireless equipment contained a mixture of old, worn clothes that Grell's people had collected from French refugees. Rough cotton and wool skirts far below the knee, blouses a few sizes too large, head scarfs—all slightly tattered in dull tones of gray and brown. The wizards of London had even seasoned the pockets with fine French lint to fool the gestapo's dogs.

I had done my best to change my appearance to play the part—dyed my hair gray, tied it in a bun above my head, and found a pair of old wire rim spectacles with a weak prescription. I had even made a trip to the dentist to acquire a mouthful of those dreadful French fillings. For all the world, I looked the part of the doddering, elderly French woman. To my agents, I was Diane. My identity papers read Marcelle Montagne.

Only one motor torpedo boat was tied up at the dock, and its wooden gangplank with pipe rail was illuminated by an overhead floodlight on a wooden pole. Silhouettes on the deck moved quickly with purpose, and at the end of the walkway, the captain stood, his hands behind his back. Three uniformed men at parade rest flanked his side.

I gave the captain my orders, he unfolded them and pointed to the cabin in silence. In that cramped and dark space, the glow of the console offered the ship's only illumination. I took a raised chair in front of a long, narrow window with a view of the bow, now black, as more shadows scurried about the deck.

The captain entered and with a crisp motion removed his hat, placed it under his arm, and nodded toward me as he approached the panel. "Well, welcome aboard, Diane. We'll try to make it an uneventful evening for you, but Jerry may have other plans." The captain glanced at his watch and began to flip switches and turn dials on the console. He had a starched intensity about him. Precise. No-nonsense.

"Our latest intelligence reports say we may have a chance encounter near the coast of Brittany. Jerry has the advantage in weaponry, but we have speed." His voice trailed off as he regained focus on the panel and began lifting and lowering switches and checking gauges. After a few minutes, he turned a key that started a low rumble and brought the ship to life. Swiveling toward me he seemed re-energized. "I love the hunt, but tonight, well, it seems we will be the hunted."

The captain stood and, looking down at his wrist, muttered, "Where *is* your partner? We can't miss the tide."

His question wasn't aimed at me. Or was it?

"We'll travel at full speed for about two hours, 'til we're a few miles from shore," he said, pointing into the dark, "and slow to a quarter to avoid waking the enemy. Then off you go in a small dinghy for a dash to the beach. Your footprints will be washed from the sand by the rising tide."

We waited in an uncomfortable silence.

The Captain walked to the cabin door, then turned around. "Your partner," he said, "is late."

I hadn't reached out to Aramis before our scheduled departure, but I wasn't his babysitter, for Christ's sake. I suppose I could have made a call, but I'm not used to working with anyone else. I find partners irritating. They always seemed get in the way and this fellow Aramis already fit that pattern.

Ten minutes later, the captain entered the cabin with a squat bald man in tow, who could only be Aramis. I usually gain a first impression through sight, but this time was different. My first assessment was earned through smell: burnt tobacco and stale beer. As the captain approached the lighted console, he glared at me.

"I was avoidably delayed," Aramis said, groping for an empty high chair. "I made a quick stop," he said. "One for courage."

I didn't believe he was drunk. But at that moment, it wasn't the tavern call nor his tardiness, as inexcusable as it was, that bothered me. No, what offended me most was his lack of fortitude and his reprehensible lack of guile. He could have been clever about it all, made up some plausible lie—even an amusing joke, for God's sake— to demonstrate some spirit, some style. Instead, he showed himself something of a buffoon.

I'd just met my new partner, so to appear agreeable, I ignored his boorishness, stuck out my right hand and introduced myself as Diane.

"Aramis," he said, meeting mine with his own. "But you can call me Henry. Henry Laussacq."

I was appalled. He'd greeted me in true name.

Some might have thought it too early to judge a new partner, but I had no apologies to make. Aramis looked the part of a peasant, I granted him that. His plump balding head, his face with three days of white stubble, and a respectable pencil-thin moustache above his narrow upper lip—all of it was authentically French. His dress was right too. Over his gray cotton shirt, he wore a tweed coat missing a few buttons and was worn at the end of his sleeves. He looked and smelled every bit the part of my companion. But still, I couldn't help thinking him an oaf.

As the captain guided the craft past the rock jetties at the harbor's entrance and into open water, I tried to ignore Aramis, but he continued to talk—about his life in Pittsburgh, his work as a commercial artist, his experience in the First World War. Some people talked to relieve the tension and perhaps I should have been more charitable, but Aramis loved to blather for no apparent reason in a monotone, which seemed to neither quiet nor invigorate him. A soliloquy that went nowhere. Each utterance, like a leaky faucet, dripped relentlessly and inexorably, on the bare metal of my patience.

"And then Donovan brought me in. We were in the first war together, but of course, he was more highly decorated than I . . ."

Aramis quickly exceeded my limits. If I had met him on the street, I would have thought him merely a bore. But for Christ's sake, we were espionage agents, and all this personal banter reflected a distressing lack of judgment and security awareness. We were going into enemy-controlled territory. The gestapo was searching for me. I couldn't let this go on.

"Really," I said, interrupting Aramis mid-sentence. "I expect that when we reach France, you'll button it."

He turned quiet. I was sure I had wounded his pride, but that was my point. He was the inanely talkative type. I'd seem them before and I had little faith that my scolding would stick.

When the captain reached open water, he pushed the throttle forward all the way, pressing me more deeply into my padded seat. Aramis stayed silent, thankfully, and the low hum of the motor and gentle motion of the boat in that dark space gave my mind room to wander.

I thought of my most recent letter to Mother, telling her in vague terms of my new assignment. The missive had been anything but maudlin, but I had written it mindful of what Donovan had said about the dangers ahead and had realized that the sheet of paper might be the final remnant of my life. So I'd reminisced, recalling how she raised me, pulled me from the mud of Gediz, and helped me to break through my cocoon of self-doubt. How she had showed me the path, how I had followed it, and how through her patience and love, I had been transformed. Now I was spreading my wings like a monarch. A whole person, focused and with purpose, about to give the performance of my life. But mostly I told my mother I was happy, engaged in the work I was meant to do. And finally, I told her to write, though we both knew I couldn't receive her letters.

I took one last look at my documents before folding them back into my pocket. Marcelle Montagne. That single piece of paper, my changed appearance, and my wits—that was all, the thin margin, protecting me from the gestapo. And for this performance, I pulled out the old shell brooch that lay in the buttoned compartment of my purse and affixed it to my tattered overcoat. As I touched the shell's rough edges and smooth center, I remembered that day on the beach with Emil and thought of how loss had shaped and prepared me for this moment.

Now I was backstage just before the curtain was about to rise on this, the greatest act of my life.

CHAPTER SIXTEEN

Reopen correspondence with Mrs. Hall. If Virginia is killed, tell her mother immediately; if arrested or missing, tell her she's all right.

Captain William Grell

MARCH 1944, THE COAST OF BRITTANY

W e're near the drop-off point," the captain said in a low voice. "Time to get on deck. The Nez Rouge is straight ahead."

Opening the door, I was met by an icy gust that nearly blew off my headscarf. I reached for the rail and looked up. Through the strands of hair that swept across my face, I caught the first glimpse of land, a thin crust of dark coastline directly above the bow.

I grabbed the string holding my cotton headscarf in place and with the other, took the steady hand of the oarsman. My two suitcases, wireless and clothes, followed.

Aramis refused the oarsman's hand only to lunge for it when another frigid blast threatened to knock him from the deck. Seated next to me in the dinghy, he began mumbling to no one in particular something ridiculous about the weather, the early hour, or the darkness. He had no takers.

The oarsman began to stare. Patrolling German E-boats would be listening for sounds amplified by the water. Still, he kept nattering to himself until the oarsmen, spoke up, "Shut your pie-hole, mate." The chatter stopped.

Soon the rising sun would lift the curtain, but for now, we were three shadows gliding over a channel as opaque as coal and silent except for the sound of oars and water lapping on wood. I sat on my hands and shut my eyes in defense of the cold.

My eyes were closed for only a moment, and when they opened, only the silhouette of land was visible. We eased our way around the barrier rocks that broke the surf and traversed the swirling eddies until the sandy bottom came into view and our boat ground to a halt.

"This is your stop," the oarsman said, speaking in a whisper. As I lifted my leg over the gunnel, Aramis went to the prow, placed his right foot on the pointed edge and leaped out, presumably enacting in his own mind the scene of an explorer founding a new land. It was a childish act. His left leg didn't make it over. He tripped and tumbled out of the boat onto sand littered with rocks.

I ignored his grunts and muted epithets and accepted the hand of the oarsman, then my bags that I'd tucked under the bench. As they pushed off, I wished the officers Godspeed and looked to Aramis, already on his way, limping toward a quick flash of light from our reception committee. With the first rays breaking through the low clouds in front of us, I struggled across the wet sand, then up the berm of loose grey rock and black seaweed pushed ashore by the waves. Uneven terrain, two suitcases, and bulky elderly women's clothing all conspired in low light to delay my progress. Worse yet, the smooth stones of the incline caused me to wobble and slide backward, and I put my bags down momentarily to catch myself. For once, Cuthbert was useful. I planted him like a post behind me as I trudged slowly up and over the rocky incline, bags in hand, sideways.

Struggling to gain my balance, I looked up to see a hunched old gentleman with a black beret and a slender boy with a swimmer's body wave us to the edge of a tidal river that in low tide offered a smooth path from the sea. I was grateful that they met us halfway and took our bags to the cargo truck on a hard-packed road. We'd be taking the 6:53 a.m. train to Paris, where Aramis and I would look for the home of our contact, Madame Long.

As the truck's gears ground, then lurched into second and third, I found a coarse wool blanket and settled into the hay. Aramis already was snoring, but I was too excited—thoughts of France with all the possibilities and dangers that lay ahead. OSS chief Donovan had said the gestapo was still hunting me. I supposed that was true. Was my disguise good enough? And now this unexploded landmine of a man, Aramis. Would his appalling lack of judgment be our undoing? He was unlikely to change his talkative ways, that much I knew. I'd need to make adjustments to protect myself, but I hadn't reached any conclusions on just how to do it. For now, comfortable in my blanket, contented to just to be in France and watch the passing scene from the back of the truck.

It wasn't long before we approached the outskirts of town. Old women draped in black were making their way to the cathedral for Morning Prayer. I studied how they carried themselves, how they trudged up the stone steps, stooped forward as if their shoulders were carrying the weight of the world. Then more townspeople emerged walking, riding bicycles, sweeping the gutter clean with whisk brooms, and we passed under an ancient aqueduct that towered above the village of what I assumed was Morlaix.

Near the city center, I banged the wall of the bay, woke Aramis, and shouted, "*Arreter!*" We had to be near the station, and being mindful of what awaits those who arrive too early, I'd decided it was time for us to walk.

Aramis mumbled something about how early it was. The neighbor lowered the gate. We said our good-byes and began our march into town.

The train from Morlaix to Paris was filled with starched German soldiers, and while they looked our way, they paid little attention to this elderly couple on their way to Sacre Coeur to visit grandchildren. We pulled into Gare du Nord and doddered off the train onto the broad avenues of Paris.

The city was just as I remembered but also strangely different. It was like returning to your home after your parents had died only to find that someone else had moved in. The buildings still had their shabby elegance, and the fountains still flowed, but now the red and black fluttered everywhere. It seemed that the Germans, insecure about their worthiness, had to lift their leg on every building and lamppost in town.

I knew where we were going. Madame Long's home was on Rue de Babylone a short, narrow street, one of many in the seventh district that all looked alike. But within a few moments, it was clear that I'd lost my bearings. I didn't dare pull out a map. We had to muddle through, walk with purpose and fix momentarily but not too obviously on the blue street signs that began and ended each road. We continued our march until, thankfully, a landmark came into view, a tall grand structure—the barracks of the French Guards—around the corner from Madame's residence.

Though he was limping, Aramis didn't complain, but as we approached the barracks swarming with police, Aramis couldn't contain himself. "Look!" he bellowed, nudging me in the side.

I prayed to God he'd stay quiet, but what was he nattering about this time? Then I saw it. There on the wall of the station, a soiled poster with the drawing of a woman's face. *La Dame Qui Boite*, it read, is most dangerous Allied spy. We must find and destroy her.

My God! Gubbins and Donovan had been right. I was a wanted woman. Still, the notice and unflattering sketch was tattered. I thought they would have stopped looking by now. I suppose I'd still be a prize catch for some young aggressive gestapo officer looking to make a name for himself. I looked straight ahead and kept walking. Faster. As fast as Cuthbert would allow without revealing himself. It had been over year since I'd left France.

Aramis was falling behind.

I waited at the curb for Aramis to catch up.

"Was that you?" he asked.

"Shut up and keep walking," I muttered, crossing the street. When Aramis tried to engage me again, I cut him short. "Drop it," I said. And for now, he did.

Farther down on Rue de Babylone we found Madame Long's home: narrow, three stories, concrete, with red and white flowers draped over a second story wrought iron rail. We'd stay long enough to gain our bearings, find more permanent accommodations, then contact London to say we'd begun our search for safe houses south of Paris.

Madame and I were last together during that mess in '42 when circuits were collapsing all around and SOE needed sympathetic Parisians to harbor agents and help them find safe passage over the mountains. She'd been so willing to help. But this time I had mixed feelings about involving her. Perhaps she was taking too great a risk. We were right around the corner from the Guard's barracks for God's sake, and being seen with me could get her killed. But we'd only be staying for a few days. We weren't scouting sites in Paris, just wanting a place to rest our heads and plan our next move.

The years and my concerns melted away when Madame opened the door. She looked exactly as she had before—well maintained, silver-hair, upright bearing. She was even wearing the stylish brown and white silk frock I last saw her in. Still, though she knew we were coming she looked surprised.

After an awkward silence, I whispered, "It's me, Marie."

A look of wonder, then sympathy crossed her face. "Marie?" she asked, examining my matronly dress and now gray hair. "Oh, yes. Of course, I'm so sorry. It's been some time, and the war has changed both of us. Come in, please."

I took her pity, silently, as a compliment and introduced Aramis. Her home, in comfortable disrepair and had the odor of an old book. The red Heriz runner below was frayed at the edges, and above, a brown water stain looked like the continent of Australia.

She took my left elbow like an old friend, and led me down the hall. Behind us, Aramis began to burble about the oils and etchings that climbed in rows up both sides of the dull whitewashed walls.

We spoke in generalities about our last contact, when she had hidden Jeanine from the gestapo. This time it would be different, I said in tones meant to reassure. Just two nights.

"You must stay longer," Madame replied. I'm sure she meant it, but a longer stay might arouse suspicion, and with those posters still scattered about town, it was best to quickly move on.

Arriving at the old wooden banister at the end of the hall, she pointed up. "Your room is on the right, the lilac room at the other end, and your companion may stay here near the kitchen."

I thanked her. Aramis, bursting at the seams, appeared eager to engage Madame about her artwork and spew forth about the painters he knew.

My room, papered in purple and pink blossoms, was dwarfed by an ornately carved oak bed with four posts. Up since one a.m., I was too exhausted to notice the room's other appointments other than the one that mattered most, the thick straw mattress and thick goose feather comforter. As my suitcases dropped to the floor, I collapsed. I didn't care about Cuthbert and his crankiness, nor did I consider the police just around the corner. Paralyzed by weariness and the depth of the duvet, I was content to drift off. But it couldn't have been more than a few minutes when I heard a rap at the door.

It was Madame Long. "You may stay for one night," she said angrily, "and you must promise never to bring that man to this house again." Her voice cracked, and she glared at me with moistened eyes. "He told me he was an American espionage agent on his first mission in France, looking for a house for American soldiers and landing zones for airplanes. I do not know this man, and yet he opened himself so fully to me, a stranger." Her eyes were fixed and she spoke with fire. "Maybe I do not remember you as I thought. Maybe the gestapo is now outside my door. No," she said pointing at me, "this man talks too much. He must leave. On this, there can be no debate."

I tried to calm Madame Long, but there was little I could say other than apologize and tell her that, yes, I understood and we'd depart the next morning. After she left, I went downstairs to speak with Aramis.

I found him seated on his bed with his back to the door. His face was reflected in the mirror above his dresser. With deliberate silence, I entered, placed my hand on the glass knob behind my back, and pushed the door slowly until it clicked. If my eyes were hot pokers, they would have seared through his flesh. I struggled to keep my voice low.

"Aramis," I said, in a forceful whisper. "*Goddammit*. Madame Long would be hanging from a meat hook if the gestapo knew she was hiding us. If you can't keep our secrets safe, how can people trust us to keep theirs? Think, damn it, before you open that trap or yours, or you'll get all of us killed."

Aramis shrugged. Refused to be contrite. He started chatting aimlessly before coming forward with a solid sentence. He said I was blowing things out of proportion, then continued rambling.

My inner reserve melted away. "Aramis," I said, raising my voice beyond what I intended. "Stop your goddam nattering and listen. You upset Madame Long, and now she wants us out the door tomorrow."

He fell silent, then mumbled that he didn't know what he'd said that troubled her.

I hoped to God he was lying but wasn't entirely sure. That night I decided. It was much too dangerous to be tied to this chattering fool.

The next day we left Madame Long's residence. Still fuming but controlled, I told Aramis I was heading south to Creuse alone, to set up a communications post and search for landing zones near what had been the demarcation line. I'd contact him after I was settled. Aramis objected, but I replied that it wasn't safe for us to be together. The gestapo and German intelligence would be tracking my radio signals, and he would be endangered needlessly if he stayed with me. His mission would be to search for safe houses around Paris.

I was sure he thought I was abandoning him, and in truth I was, but I told him we'd continue the Saint mission—locating landing zones and safe houses—separately and communicate with each other via courier. He begged to come with me to Creuse just this once and promised he'd return to Paris the following day.

I don't know why I relented. Just being with him made my skin crawl. Who else might he reveal our mission to? God knows, I didn't have a soft spot for many people, much less idiots, but there were so few OSS agents in the field. Maybe I'd offer some last-minute guidance before sending him out into a dangerous world on his own. And for better or worse, he'd need to know where I'd set up the letterbox for his courier. So I allowed Aramis to accompany me to Creuse. But only for the day. Then he'd return to Paris. Which he did.

A London contact, farmer Eugene Lopinat, offered a modest accommodation in Creuse—a sparsely furnished one-room tenant's house without electricity or running water. It was isolated on a dusty road just outside the village, and that's where I began my work. In return for room and board, I took Lopinat's black and white Holsteins to pasture and cooked simple meals for him and his elderly mother over a large blackened fieldstone fireplace in the main house. The farmer became my sponsor, introducing me casually to his neighbors, allowing me to gain their trust as I searched for level and secluded landing spots in their fields. Many of Lopinat's neighbors sensed the war's tide turning and signed up for Lysander receptions.

The tenant's house was just large enough to lay out my long wire antenna, but without electricity, I powered the radio using a bicycle on a wooden platform rigged to an old generator. I'd pedal enough to get the generator running, then start my transmission. My first session, I told London that Aramis and I were safely in place and offered code names for drop zone locations and townspeople, trustworthy and willing to help.

Despite my demand that Aramis use couriers, he couldn't keep his promise to stay away. Three visits in April alone. Each time, I scolded him and made it clear that he wasn't welcome, but it was no use. Maybe he hadn't been properly trained to use couriers—clearly, he was oblivious to good security practices, and acted like a lonely lap dog looking for praise. I did recognize his few successes, as small as they were.

Aramis had set up a letterbox on Rue de Richeleau in Paris, and on his third visit, he seemed particularly excited—he'd found an old friend, a Monsieur Rabut, who could help. "My good friend, Pierre, said we can use his house as a hideout for two or three."

Bravo, Aramis. I commended his minor achievement but found curious the word he used to describe it. He called it a "hideout." It was as if we were abetting Hollywood gangsters evading the law. In his eyes, maybe all this was a game of cops and robbers.

His regular visits became alarming. There were Germans in the area, and he started to become chummy with the farmer. One of us had to go.

I reported the safe house Aramis had found on 46 Rue Danzig to London, offered a codename for it, and established the password needed to gain entrance. But by mid-April, barely a month after we had arrived, the Saint mission began wrapping up.

I was restless and unwilling to hang around babysitting both Aramis and the safe houses. In truth, my work in Creuse was finished. I'd already found a safe house north of Creuse, landing zones and had organized reception committees. It was time to spread my wings.

One of my most trusted agents, Louis, a fearless but gentle man with biceps and a neck like a prize fighter, took me aside. It was a warm spring day, and he'd caught on that I was restless. "There are a hundred men hiding in the hills north in Cosne," he said, lightly touching my shoulder. "They are wanted by the gestapo. Hunted men, who have desire but no weapons to fight the Germans."

"Where are these maquis?" I asked.

"My wife Mimi's father, Captain Vessereau, who heads the gendarme in Cosne," Louis said with pride, "knows the mountain path just outside of town."

That night I told London my plan to move on. London believed my story that lack of electricity made Creuse a poor location for wireless work and agreed with my plan to move farther north across the demarcation line into what had been the German occupied zone. When their reply came, it made my heart race. They agreed.

"Proceed to Cosne with caution," London said. "The area is very hot."

Perhaps it was wrong not to tell Aramis that I was leaving town, much less offer a forwarding address, but it was for the best. He'd shown that he couldn't be trusted, and if given the opportunity, he'd try to tag along, and one of his indiscrete mumblings would get both of us killed. Besides, I refused to work with people I couldn't trust. It was a shortcoming of mine, being short-tempered and bull-headed, but I preferred to work alone. Still, I'd never understand why OSS had chosen Aramis to lead Saint. But all of that didn't matter now. I was free of him, on my own as I had planned, and that was an exhilarating thought.

Aramis would stay put in Paris, where he'd be responsible for himself and mind the letterbox and a few safe houses. A small job that would require the full range of his ability. For now, I'd still support Saint as a pianist through my courier, Madame Rabut, the wife of Aramis's friend, but I made her promise not to reveal my new location in the Cosne to anyone—especially Aramis.

I'm sure my old partner was angry that I'd abandoned him, but he couldn't have been sore for long. I later received a letter from Madame Long making amends and saying she had spotted Aramis painting by the Seine. In my eyes, both of us had gotten what we wanted. He was in Paris painting, and after nearly two long years, I was working my way back to the heart of France. It was as I had hoped—now I was responsible only for myself, carving out a mission as a free agent, working where I could do some good. And there was so much left to do.

*   *   *

Louis told Captain Vessereau that I was coming, and after a long bus ride down country roads, around fields and through forests, I reached the small town of Cosne on the east bank of the Loire. There I found the captain, a proud man with a face wrinkled like an old handbag and basset hound eyes, seated in his cramped office in the back of the town hall. I introduced myself as Diane.

"Tell me," he said, "what news did you bring me of Louis and Mimi?"

"Your son-in-law is doing the work of five," I said. "Louis oversees recruiting, and when the time comes for planes to drop men and weapons from the sky, Creuse will be ready to play its part in the liberation of France. And Mimi," I said smiling, "was the best courier I've ever had, clever and unafraid."

Vessereau smiled broadly. It was the only time I recall the corners of his eyes lifting, and even then, it was only for an instant.

"Captain Vessereau," I said, "now we must speak of Cosne."

"Our numbers are growing, over one hundred and seventy, and the Nazis and their stooges know the maquis will fight if given the chance," Vessereau offered. His speech was slow and dry. He didn't seem to notice when a drop of snow white spittle flew from his mouth.

"Diane," he said, "Cosne is a small town, but we have our own spies. They tell me where the secret police are searching for the maquis in the hills." The captain looked down and threw his right arm into the air in resignation. "But without the means to free ourselves, there is so little we can do but hide."

I told him that I could help, and he looked up, hopefully, though I couldn't expect him to believe me. Not yet.

"I'll need a place, several places, safe to work," I said, "and men we can trust to catch the leather canisters that fall from the sky."

He brightened. "Everything I have is yours," he said eagerly, and then mentioned that for the time being, I could board with him and his wife. "No one will suspect the attic of the Captain of the Gendarme," he said, "as the residence of an Allied agent."

He then rose and held my outstretched hand. His voice softened, and his eyes looked especially sorrowful. "Diane, these men hiding in the hills are commoners—farmers, shop owners, tradesmen—they have lived in despair for so long. Some have turned bitter waiting for help. Others will be fearful now that it has come. All we ask is that you give us the tools for our liberation. We will find a way to do the rest."

It was late in the evening, and as I unfurled the antenna to my radio in Vessereau's barn, the full weight of his words weighed on me. This small box, my skill, London's response. So much was riding on each link of this fragile chain. In dots and dashes, I gave my call sign—the coded phrase London used to confirm my identity. Some pianists used a snippet from a favorite Bible verse, others used a bit of poetry. My call sign was a line from the Greek myth Pandora. I'd loved that story so, growing up in the fields that surrounded our family's farm:

**Then she opened the box a second time and out flew
a butterfly named Hope.**

It was far beyond my scheduled reporting time, and I was about
to give up for the evening, when a faint scratch in the airways came
from a long distance, maybe from across the channel. It was like a
small flame that needed breath to keep it alive, and I tapped out a
short response. It was London. As the flame grew, I began my coded
message requesting a drop—a double load for Vessereau's maquis,
which I called the Licensee circuit. Sten guns, each with 300 rounds
of 9mm Parabellum; carbines; Mills grenades; field dressings—all of
it. London copied and said the drop would come soon, possibly at the
next full moon in five days' time.

Plan Vert, the Allies' coordinated plan for sabotage operations to
support D-Day, was approaching just as Donovan had said. When
the signal was given, the maquis of Licensee would play their part,
come down from the hills to cut railway and telephone lines, destroy
the train station, locomotives and rolling stock—anything in the area
that could support Germany's defense of the continent. We'd help
sever the body from the head. Reinforcements could never be allowed
to reach the beachfront where the Allies were to come ashore. But our
maquis needed the equipment drop and weapons training before we
could play our part. I made our request to London, then I padded my
list by adding 145 pounds of plastic explosives, detonators, charges,
and money to buy the support of those who wouldn't give it freely.

I was all ears. I made damn sure I didn't miss a nightly schedule
and waited impatiently, with headphones on, for the signal that
supply planes were on the way. And I listened to BBC for fresh news
of Plan Vert.

*   *   *

The weather that spring was dreadful—heavy clouds, fog, cold
drizzle, hard rain. Many flights were scrubbed, and aircraft that did
fly often dropped their loads far wide of mark. I was never so glad as
when the clouds lifted just long enough in early May for us to catch

the parachutes shimmering in the damp moonlight. Only three of our thirteen leather canisters were lost.

There was much work left to support Licensee, now over two hundred men. Vessereau, my second, distributed the arms. Together we planned the target list with London's guidance. Our top priority was the train station at Cosne and its network of communications lines, which like a bundle of nerves, carried vital messages throughout the corpus and up to the head, Paris.

The captain had been around weapons all his life and quickly mastered the simple Sten but knew less about how to train men. But he had their trust and the good judgment to pick from his gendarmes the most skilled among them to serve as trainers. The ranks of the maquis swelled and we divided the corps into nine groups of twenty-five. As they continued to prepare, I traveled to the south for a few days. Antelme, now the leader of a revived Ventriloquist circuit, needed wireless support after his pianist was shot dead, found by gestapo troops hunting wireless signals in their direction-finding vans.

When I returned a few days later to the town hall in Cosne, I found the captain with his head bowed, his elbows on his knees, and his eyes fixed inches from his desktop. A few drops lay on the desk. He knew I was there only a few feet away, but he didn't speak until I asked what was wrong.

"Louis has been arrested," he said in a whisper that cracked.

The gestapo had been especially active that spring, taking out leaders of the resistance, working to disrupt the growing number of circuits. The Germans, sensing their grasp on France slipping away, had become more ruthless, pressuring their spies and informers to gather the information they'd need to counter the massive Allied attack everyone knew was coming.

I told Vessereau that I'd ask London for any information they might have on Louis, his condition and whereabouts, but we both understood that nothing could be done to help him. Louis was in gestapo hands, and now our focus had to be on the living. It was unspoken but unmistakable. Louis would be tortured without mercy, and we had to assume he would give up what he knew: at very least, our identities and location.

"We'll need to get you and your men farther into the hills," I said.

Over the next few days, I pieced together Louis's story—part of it came from CE in London, and some came from informants in Creuse. It seemed that Louis had been captured by a German agent, Filias, posing as an SOE officer. The gentle giant had been seen on a stretcher, bloodied, and loaded onto a train headed for Dachau. I offered the captain a glimmer of hope, telling him I'd heard of prison escapes, but we knew the odds were long. He'd probably never see Louis again.

MAY 1944, COSNE

The two-day rule. The most you can hope for is forty-eight hours; then you must expect the gestapo's knock on the door. In my world, you assumed everyone cracked under torture. After learning of Louis's misfortune and offering a quick condolence, I told Vessereau the countdown had begun. He needed to pack his rucksack and Sten and make his way into the woods. Though he nodded in agreement, his movements were sluggish. I'm sure his mind was spinning, weighed down with worry, not having heard from Mimi. But now his responsibility was to his men. I told him I'd been in his shoes. It was a hard message but the captain had to hear it.

"You have to choke down your sorrow and save your strength for the living."

Day two it was my turn. I awoke to a DF aircraft buzzing overhead, and Sophie, one of my young, more excitable informants, was beating on my door, yelling, breathlessly, "The gestapo is coming!" She'd seen from her third-floor window the dust kick up from three Black Marias speeding toward the house. They'd be at the door in minutes.

I had doubts I'd escape in time but was determined not to let them win. I grabbed my wireless and hobbled down those narrow, creaky attic stairs as fast as Cuthbert would take me. He was thick-witted that morning but fully harnessed, and we made it to the thick hedgerow across the street just in time to see the gestapo, guns drawn, rush the house. My heart was thumping. I swear it almost leaped from my chest as I laid there, still, until the men in black uniforms roared off. I had told no one where I was headed next—down the road five kilometers to the farm of the captain's trusted friend, Jules Juttry.

Monsieur Juttry, a crusty old gentleman with a limp acquired in the Great War, welcomed me into his modest frame home with a large fieldstone fireplace and told me I could set up my radio on his kitchen table. I told him plainly that was a foolish idea. I shouldn't have phrased it so bluntly, but sensing his embarrassment, I followed up more gently, saying that if direction-finding aircraft found my signal, they would bomb his home. It was more prudent for me to take up residence in his barn's loft, where he could plausibly deny knowing my activities.

*   *   *

Allied bombers had been pounding the coast of France all during the spring of 1944, and circuit operators and resistance leaders alike knew the invasion could come at any time. Nine p.m. became our sacred hour when crystal radio sets were tuned to the BBC. Between the news and the weather, we waited impatiently to hear: "London calling. Personal messages for our friends in occupied countries." We'd sort through the program's outwardly trivial and nonsensical musings: Mrs. Smith in Doncaster needs to contact her family in Hull. The Trojan War will not be held. John is growing a very long beard this week. Mixed with snippets of prose and poetry, each message held a secret meaning.

We waited impatiently for two very special BBC messages. The first would tell us to get ready to attack. Then a second message would come, perhaps the next day or the next week or a week after that, ordering us to execute our sabotage mission, Plan Vert—signaling the beginning of the D-Day invasion.

The Germans knew that BBC messages were the clarion call for unleashing the Allied assault but they couldn't unravel the secrets, so they tried, in desperation, to block our reception. It became a crime to listen to what they called, the BBC's "anti-nationalist propaganda," but it was a futile attempt. It couldn't be enforced. The Wehrmacht had more success cutting electricity in Cosne and jamming broadcasts by transmitting on the radio stations' frequency.

We all knew this whole invasion business was a massive gamble. All the Allies' chips were on the table, and as the days grew closer to the all-out assault, everyone's emotions frayed. I snapped at Vessereau. His men didn't have enough discipline. They needed more training. Vessereau snapped back. He was doing all he and his men could. They would be ready.

London had only told us about our part of Plan Vert. Without knowing the bigger picture, we felt alone. Most of us acted with faith the Allies would prevail, but then the weather turned bad. Cold wind, more rain. Our mood soured. No one was confident how D-Day would play out.

But London ruled the airways the night of June first 1944. Breaking through German radio jamming, using several broadcasting bands, BBC announcers issued the first message, coded as a Verlaine poem:

**Les sanglots/ longs des violins/ de l'automne.
The long sobs of the violins of autumn.**

London's use of poetry, as maudlin as it was, set in motion the final phase of the war. But at that moment, I wasn't thinking of verse. I felt relief. The "get-ready" message had finally arrived. D-Day was coming.

In truth, we'd been ready for some time, and that snippet of poetry only seemed to heighten the maquis' nervousness. Some were anxious the final order would come too quickly, and others were fearful it would never arrive. I heard it in their laugh and saw it in their eyes— how they looked around then lingered on the faces of their friends and comrades. They were checking the odds and placing their bets. Gabriel, or Clement, or Gaspard. Who would fall? Then a stricken look. A terrifying final thought. Could it be me?

With the invasion inching closer, some of the maquis swung to superstition, others to God. Like prize fighters in the ring, they sparred more intensely now among themselves, readying their weapons and steeling their minds, while imagining the massing of troops across the channel. And the maquis knew their mission. German reinforcements could never be allowed to reach the front. After all their concern, all their worry, the maquis would settle on one comforting thought. We're in this fight together.

I confess, doubts seeped onto my mind the night of the first signal. Usually, I can push it all away but the movie reel in my head wouldn't let me sleep. Hundreds of young bodies, bloated and bobbing in the brine. Not a premonition. A memory of Dieppe. So many, hundreds, of lovely Canadian and British boys scattered on the beach; their legs rolling gently to the small waves washing ashore, amidst the screeching gulls and the bright blue and white above.

Then I thought of Jeanine and Alesh. My mouth grew dry and for a moment, I lost my breath. Maybe the Germans had advanced warning of D-Day too.

*   *   *

Most of us were insufferable, waiting for that second message. One day passed, then another, and another. During those days, the weather stayed foul, and we were certain the downpour and low ceiling were the reason for the delay. As we huddled under canopies, the only sound was the muffled drops on the tarp, then the downpour around us. Even if we didn't say it, we all thought, shit, let's just get on with it. No matter what. The wait was unbearable. But those early days, no signal came. Unbearable nothing.

As we began to question what we'd heard, on the night of the fifth of June, the BBC came on the air with the words we were waiting for:

Blessent mon Coeur d'une languerur monotome— Wound my heart with monotonous languor.

Le Jour J—D-Day—had arrived.

CHAPTER SEVENTEEN

———

Dear Mrs. Hall,
Thank you so much for your letter addressed to your daughter
Virginia. I am sorry to hear you have been ill and I fully realize
how upsetting Virginia's silence must have been.

You must not worry. Virginia is doing a spectacular, man-sized
job.

> *Sincerely,*
> *Charlotte Norris*
> *For the Commanding Officer*
> *1ˢᵗ Experimental Detachment*

JUNE 1944, COSNE, FRANCE

I was in the barn's loft when the signal arrived. I clambered down
the wooden ladder to meet Vessereau at our usual meeting spot at
the edge of the woods.

"The time has come," I said.

We hurriedly gathered our maquis in the dark. In low tones by the
light of the fire and using a stick in the dirt, I reviewed our mission one
last time: Destroy the communications and railroad from Cosne that
traveled up the spine of France to the head, Paris. First, we'd secure

then blow the station and communications center, then the side yards with its locomotives and rolling stock. And before retreating into the woods, we'd set charges to the rails. As our fighters assembled into groups, I took Vessereau aside and said Cuthbert would slow us down. He understood the plan better than anyone. I'd stay back in fringe of the woods to direct the operation.

In stealth, the men and women of the circuit Licensee made their way through the woods toward the station. The first group, crouching low, crossed the tracks and entered the building, where Vessereau later said they'd found the station master in cramped quarters with his forehead on his desk, asleep. A stroke of good luck. Two men masked in charcoal held him from behind and covered his mouth, his eyes opened wide with terror. He would be released, his captors said, but only after revealing where the German sentries were posted.

He pointed nervously to the back of the station, and that's where the group of three were found, unaware, smoking. They were dispatched quickly with a short burst of automatic fire, even as their cigarettes' white cloud hung still in the cool night air. Two other soldiers walking up the platform came running, guns drawn, but met a larger force of maquis. They shared the fate of their comrades.

For the next hour, orange flashes and the pop of gunfire filled the night air, but none of these sights or sounds were sustained. It seemed we had far greater numbers, and our maquis worked as a team to quickly overcome the German sentries.

The station secure, other silhouettes moved swiftly in the night, weaving around, over, into, and under the locomotives and rolling stock. I imagined them attaching the plastic explosives and detonators to the boilers and axles and watched them climbed the stanchions elevating the telephone and telegraph wires. Silhouettes huddled over rails attached devices that later would detonate under the weight of arriving trains. The rails would take a week to mend. And the locomotives with cracked boilers and engine blocks? The men had so much plastic with them, I told Vessereau the locomotives would never be repaired.

The mission complete, the maquis fell back into the woods. All of us sensed the pressure from the blasts from behind, and in front our shadows flickered against an orange background. With each explosion, a wild cheer would rise up from the maquis for what they'd done and for the time we'd bought the boys on the beach.

The men were so filled with bravado. The Marseillaise mixed with drunk laughter echoed late into the night. For now, they'd savor the win, their first. Tomorrow or the next day or the day after that, when the Germans counterattacked, the men and women of Licensee would learn that the easy fighting was behind them. This maquis of bakers, tailors, and shopkeepers wouldn't know how sweet victory could be without suffering for it, and violent deaths within their ranks would come soon enough.

But I wouldn't be there to help them. London had agreed that it was time for me to move on. With the gloves off and sabotage operations finally underway, there were more maquis in the surrounding hills to arm and organize. Vessereau turned silent when I told him it was time for me to leave, but I added quickly that my replacement, Leon, would arrive by Lysander in two weeks' time to support his maquis just as I had. He nodded, but I saw the disappointment on his face. It would be difficult for Vessereau to say goodbye and wait for another organizer he didn't know or yet trust. And I didn't talk about my next assignment. The big job London said they had waiting for me.

London had agreed to what I wanted all along. I was to establish the Saint circuit in my old home base, the Haute Loire.

JULY 1944, CHAMBON SUR LIGNON

The Haute Loire. It was what I'd dreamt about since my escape from France in '42. Thoughts of my return had lifted me from the unrelenting ennui of Madrid and its dreadful heat, kept me focused, and drove my return to London. But then roadblocks had been thrown up: Buck said no. Gubbins said too dangerous. OSS hesitated. But Donovan, without seasoned spies in France, was in a bind. He offered a small mission, I'd be the radio operator for Aramis, and I said yes.

But I had other plans, did what was expected then expanded my charter like I'd done before. I'd moved on, claimed a roving mission for myself, just me, and showed OSS I could do the job by organizing the maquis, hundreds of them, along the way. Now my wish had been granted. I was in Haute Loire, where I'd organize hundreds more for sabotage operations to make sure the boys on the shore stayed alive and got back home in one piece. Vindicated and ready. I felt complete.

But the Haute Loire brought deeply unsettling memories, too. I'd be returning to the lair of that monster, Barbie, and Place Bellecour, too, where he's strung up the mutilated bodies of spies and innocents side by side on metal hooks for all to see. And the danger now was greater, still. As the boys were pushing off the beach the Butcher of Lyon and his cronies were growing more evil and vindictive. The Allies' attack stung and enraged Barbie so that he had locked a hundred teenagers in a nearby school house, then burned it down.

Returning to Haute Loire would exhume other unsettling memories—leaving in the middle of the night with few words for Guerin, Rousset, Bertillon, and my other agents. How I had neglected my first responsibility, their protection. Where were they in all this mess? Were they still alive? No time yet to look.

*   *   *

When London had said I'd be returning to the Haute Loire, I had tapped out a message to the local maquis leader, Jacques Monier, to say I was coming. But it was London's closing query that had caught me off guard. They asked, have you heard from Aramis?

Aramis, that indiscreet boor, of all people. I told London we'd gone our separate ways long ago, and he'd made no effort to contact me. That was stretching the truth because, in all honesty, I hadn't provided Aramis with any forwarding address. Then they had the gall to ask if I could use him in Haute Loire. My response was a quick NO.

I made my way across the old demarcation line into the Haute Loire and the hills around Chambon sur Lignon where London said Monier was holed up with several thousand maquis without arms. It was the fourteenth of July, and carrying nothing more than my two leather suitcases, I met up with the maquis in the woods due east of the regional capital, Le Puy.

The maquis were little more than schoolboys in worn clothes and dirty faces, yet they seemed to have a playful spirit about them. Good young men with stout hearts. Now that the invasion forces were moving swiftly south and east, the tide was turning, and the maquis' ranks were swelling with untrained men armed only with hatred and hope.

Though I had written Monier of my intended arrival, when I entered the camp, the leader was nowhere to be found. Instead, I was met by a public shouting match on the brink of breaking into a brawl. A narrow-faced man with a pointed nose was taking the brunt of it from four scrubby men of diminutive stature. They weren't arguing about the strategy of war; it was about money.

I stepped into their circle and lowered my bags but was ignored until I made my presence known. "Which one of you is in charge?" I demanded.

The uproar stopped, and each turned to me almost in unison. They looked shocked, probably by the audacity of a woman, a dowdy looking gray-haired woman, breaking into such an august klatch of youthful, self-important men.

The most detestable one, a short piggish man with wild black eyebrows, a low forehead, and blunt features, whom I'd heard was called Gevold, spoke up. "And who the hell are you?" he asked, his eyes wide with fire.

I looked directly into the flame. "I'm Diane. The one who has the weapons and money to finance your maquis."

I didn't expect deference just then, but I did expect respect—but even that was beyond Gevold's capacity. I'd worked with men of his ilk before, bullies who take but never give.

Perhaps I had shocked them into silence, or maybe the revelation of my purpose and largess had made their argument moot, but for whatever reason, I thanked God that I had put an end to their infantile and insufferable bickering. As they retreated without the civility of an introduction, I pulled aside the tall, narrow-faced man, whom they had called Fayolle, and asked about my accommodations. As I suspected, nothing had been planned.

"You caught us off-guard," Fayolle said, weakly. "Monier, who knew of such things, had a fight with Hulet and left with his maquis a few days ago." I remained silent, wondering how I could make this work and what my host now would say to his unexpected guest.

After a moment Fayolle filled the awkwardness. "For the time being, you may stay with me and my wife."

I accepted his offer, hoping to build rapport, and stayed in their home for two nights. The first was spent tossing around on the straw bed with thoughts of the five leaders quarreling, each jealous of their own position. How in this toxic space could I hope to succeed? London had work for us, and I had no time to develop relationships with men who questioned each other's authority, let alone mine.

The second night, I went to sleep accepting the only choice I had—to build a relationship on a simple, unspoken bargain: arms for influence. My authority, granted by London, was worth little and would last only as long as I could deliver the goods.

The next week, I bicycled the region, looking for drop zones and more suitable accommodations and found both. The direction-finding aircraft with their antennas looking for rogue allied signals would be looking for me, so I moved with my wireless frequently, first into the barn of a baker in Villonge and then to the home of Madame Lebrat, whose husband was a prisoner in Germany. But I didn't stay there for long. I was looking for a remote area and found an abandoned house with three rooms and a large working space that had belonged to the Salvation Army.

It was there that I made contact with London and learned of their plans for me. It was also where I met Lt. Bob, leader of the smallest maquis in the Haute Loire. I surprised both of us when I opened the door to my fieldstone house and there he was.

Bob was not a handsome man. He was slight with eyes too narrowly spaced. But he had an open smile and a hearty laugh. "Diane," he said without introduction, "forgive me for intruding, but I had to stop by to see my new neighbor. I heard you arrived to a warm reception from the maquis." As he spoke the corners of his mouth turned upward. "Gevold and the rest are assholes, but like a fiefdom, each has their own followers, and as much as they deserve it, you cannot ignore them."

I smiled and welcomed Lt. Bob into my sparsely furnished house and took the chair near the side window, facing the front door.

"Yesterday, we received news of the German officers' plot to kill their führer," he said. "Encouraging news for us. The maquis now smells blood and are more eager to take action. But Gevold and the rest?" He shook his head. "They have visions of glory, and their squabbling will become even more insufferable."

"I heard about the plot," I said. "More men will join the maquis, but its leaders—" I sighed. "Well, I enter new relationships with few expectations. The afternoon I met Gevold and the rest, even my lowest hopes weren't realized."

Bob had an easy, attractive laugh that started low and rose on the second breath. He seemed a passionate man with a sense of humor.

"Yes, Fayolle, Gevold and the others will never have the loyalty of their men, but they're good fighters, and they can be your allies if you give them just enough of what they need."

Bob then told me his story. He had been a Broadway agent—a Frenchman trained by the British military, MI-6—who had been cast like a mustard seed on the shore of Brittany and blown by the wind to finally take root in Haute Loire. He had been in the mountains for over a year and had a small band of loyal followers. Adrift without regular supplies of weapons or a wireless, he and his men engaged in skirmishes with the Germans, but without a way to contact London, he was cut off from the larger plan.

"I have come to ask for your help," he said. "But first, you must meet my men."

As we walked side by side through his camp, Lt. Bob called out to each by name. "Jacques, come here. I'd like you to meet the newest member of our maquis," he said with a smile, turning to me.

Jacques came and saluted crisply, and Bob returned the gesture. Other men followed and soon I was encircled.

"Jacques is from Le Puy. He sold shoes before the Nazis burned down his store. Over there," Bob said, pointing, "is Antoine. He survived the massacre of innocents at Oradour-sur-Glane. And Richard," he called out, turning serious, "Where are you from, again?" As Richard approached, Bob didn't wait for a response. A big grin shot across Bob's face as he grabbed Richard's shoulder and shook it. "Richard's a city boy from Paris, a bit worldly for us peasants, but we tolerate him."

Richard gave a sheepish half-grin, as if he'd heard this story before, and Bob went around the circle and introduced me to the rest of his men. Bob had an easy way about him, and his men responded with warmth and even, dare I say, a touch of love. He presented me to his maquis as Diane.

I thanked Bob and told the men how glad I was to be in Haute Loire, how the Allies were gaining momentum, and how we'd face a stern test. But mostly I gave them my promise that working with Bob, I'd get the weapons and provide the direction they needed to rid the Haute Loire of the Nazis.

"It was a good start," Bob said as we returned to my fieldstone house. We had just entered the door's rounded arch when he pointed to my wireless set up on the table. "And what does London have in store for us?"

Silently, I went across the room to my wireless suitcase, pulled out and began to unfold a map. As it opened, Bob's eyes grew wide and intense. I was close enough to hear his breaths deepen as he focused on the circle drawn around the capital, Le Puy, and the Xs where German troops were stationed.

"Yes, I've known for some time what we must do," Bob said, understanding the map that lay before him. "But to reclaim the capital of Haute Loire so soon after the Le Jour-J?" He shook his head. "My spies tell me there are thousands of Germans in Le Puy."

Lt. Bob was right, and London understood the long odds too. We couldn't succeed in a straight up fight against the Germans in Le Puy. But still, it was our mission, and I had to make it work.

"Look," I said. "London tells me that the Allies are sweeping south and east, pushing out quicker than anyone expected. And," I said sliding my index finger across the paper, "the Nazis are in retreat. But before they reach Haute Loire, we must retake Le Puy so the people can defend themselves and deny the enemy a safe haven."

Lt. Bob paused, then nodded slowly but didn't seem convinced. His slow response told me that he understood London's strategy and the reason for its demand. But he didn't know the full story, the numbers and how heavily they were stacked against us. Still, I sensed he trusted me.

"Let it be so," he said. "But we will need more arms and men. Of course, Gevold, Hulet and the others must join." He sighed. "I do not say this lightly. You've seen these men. They do not work well among themselves, but with outsiders—especially a woman who controls the weapons they need, and was chosen by London to lead them?"

It burned me but Bob laid it on the table. These men didn't trust a woman at the top. It wasn't like there weren't women in the resistance for Christ's sake. Plenty. Maybe it was narrow-mindedness that kept so few women from joining the fighting forces of the maquis. And now it didn't matter that I had more experience in leading men in battle than all of them combined; that I'd suffered the indignity of small expectations to grow and command the most important circuit in France; that my actions had saved the lives of hundreds of their countrymen. But I didn't have time for arguments and petty chauvinism. Our mission was too important. I had to make this work.

"I'll tell Gevold and the rest I'll withhold nothing," I said. "I'll give arms to anyone willing to take Le Puy. I don't give a damn about their feelings for me personally."

"Yes," Bob said, "but please, let me speak with them. To liberate Le Puy, the odds of success are not sure, but I know the appeals and arguments that will make them join this fight."

I couldn't lie to myself: I harbored a grudge against these self-important, squabbling men. But we had to get on with it, time was ticking away, so I agreed to Bob's request.

Before he departed, Lt. Bob and I pored over the maps and worked out a plan for the maquis—how they should be divided into groups, each leader in charge of his own men at a major crossroad that ringed the city: Longogne, Retournac, and Tence. I explained that we'd stagger the destruction of rails, bridges, and roads and over several days, squeeze the city from three sides but leave an avenue for the Germans to escape.

Lt. Bob then spoke up. "I ask a favor, Diane. At this junction, the road through St. Clement," he said, pointing to a road to the north of Le Puy, "I wish to station my maquis, to attack the retreating Germans."

At first I objected. His small maquis could quickly become overrun. It was a bold request. "Bob, our combined force is a fraction of the retreating German army." I hesitated but knew how important his request was. "I'll agree only if you accept support from Fayolle and give your word that you will not engage the enemy directly, only harass him." I stood up and muttered almost as an afterthought, "You do know London says this plan to liberate Le Puy is a bluff. Our forces are so small, but it's our only chance."

He nodded silently.

*   *   *

Our plan was set, and at my next scheduled broadcast, I radioed our needs: five plane drops, over one hundred canisters containing a horde of automatic Stens, thousands of 9-mm rounds, three-inch mortars, plastic explosives—enough to blow bridges, tracks, communications posts—field dressings for the wounds that were sure to come, money, and a small pleasure, cartons of Luckys for the men.

I couldn't be certain when the planes would arrive. The RAF made excuses, true I suppose, that they were backed up, making hundreds of drops of soldiers and supplies to maquis throughout the country. But I was emphatic and made the case plainly: my acceptance as a leader was tied to these deliveries. London said they understood, but they had their priorities.

I gained the latest intelligence by slipping into Le Puy amid the German soldiers and made notes of troop positions, and the routes and times they travelled. Then I called on an old friend, the Mayor of Le Puy, Monsieur Pebellier.

The Mayor didn't recognize me when I knocked on his door, so when it opened, and saw his quizzical look, I whispered, "It's me, Virginia Hall."

He searched my face and quickly ushered me into his office. "Madame Hall," he said, smiling broadly, greeting me with three kisses and a warm embrace. "Yes, you've changed, but I have too," he said patting his stomach. "It is so good to see you. But," he began wagging his finger, "I have to question your intellect. Yes, the posters are now worn and," he said scanning my dowdy appearance, "you do not appear as you once were. But in my position, I hear things, and I hear your name still is on the butcher's lips."

I stayed silent.

The mayor pointed to two boxy chairs by his oversized desk piled high with papers. We took our seats.

"*Le Jour-J* has brought hope and fear. The soldiers and gestapo now are like mad dogs, angry their bone is being snatched from them. The reprisals, public executions, private atrocities . . ." The mayor stopped mid-sentence and looked up as if inspecting the ceiling, but in the light, the lower half of his eyes filled. "The killings happen with such frequency; the people of Le Puy cannot take much more." He looked away. "And now, of course, our colleague, Miss Bertillon…"

"Suzanne?"

"Last month I heard she received the knock at the door. Taken in the dark of night. But has she been interviewed by the gestapo? I do not know. If she had been broken, would I be here with you now? Only God can answer." He shrugged and looked at me. "Perhaps Fritz is preoccupied with the Allies."

"Monsieur Pebellier, what I tell you is of the gravest importance but you may not ask questions." Pebellier nodded silently. "You must plan for the people of Le Puy. If the city needs supplies, they must enter your city by the end of the next week."

He stayed silent, perhaps waiting for more, but that was all I would say.

"Ten days. I understand," he said, quietly. "We hear the Allies are coming. Our people have been pushed so hard by the Germans.

They are ready for whatever comes, and most will assist in their own liberation. But be warned. I hear the German general staff plans to evacuate Lyon and make Le Puy its new home, and with the senior staff will come many more soldiers."

*   *   *

Our plan was set, everyone had been told, and now I waited by my wireless for the signal that the supply planes were coming. I was hopeful that first day. Surely London knew how important this mission was. But the radio was silent, and then the second day, silence too. And from then on, the radio's stillness brought a new pressure, which built incrementally and inexorably. Each day like the turning of a screw. Nothing. I told myself that certainly by the weekend the arms would arrive.

The weekend came and went. The screw tightened. The burden grew heavier. Gevold, Hulet, and Fayolle were at my door, and I felt the presence of those who were not: Pebellier and the suffering people of Le Puy. I began to dread the knock. First silence, then questions: What have you heard? When will the planes come? When do you *think* the planes will come?

I tried to remain hopeful, but the disappointment was taking a toll. The anger flared. "Why has London abandoned us?" they'd ask. Then they'd turn away. The clock continued to tick, and I was certain the general staff would arrive in Le Puy any day now.

It was the third week of July, eight days since I'd spoken with Pebellier, when Lt. Bob showed up at my door. He'd purposely left me alone, he said, but now he had come. The tenuous bargain I'd constructed with the maquis was in tatters. I had no patience for the maquis, London, and this whole goddam mess.

"Diane," Bob said, "I come on behalf not of myself but of what I see in my men and hear from Gevold and the rest. We are ready to blow the bridge at Montagnac, cut the railroad lines at Langogne, and sever the main approaches to Le Puy, just as we planned, but . . ." Lt. Bob looked directly at me, "I tell them, trust Diane. Be patient, the weapons and explosives will come. But the other maquis, Hulet and

Gevold, they mock me for having faith in you, and my men are losing faith themselves."

"I know, goddammit!" I shouted. "But I didn't expect this from you, of all people. Every goddam night I listen for the signal that the drop is on, but every night nothing. All my time is spent waiting. London says our load is too heavy, the Haute Loire is too far south from Massingham, so the planes have to come up from North Africa. And now, all the maquis want weapons, so the drops are stacking up like cordwood all around this goddam country."

I stopped my screed. I hated losing control like that, but I'd lost patience days ago. I didn't apologize, but I did lower my voice. "Listen Bob. I've been on the wireless nightly, working my schedule, pleading with London. It's not a good answer, I know. I'm on the line here, just like you. But London is definite. The drops will come even if they have to be done in daylight." I paused, cooling. "But only God knows when. Grell promised arms and men—a Jedburgh Team, codenamed Jeremy—to parachute in and help with the attack. But we're at the mercy of London's blasted schedule for that, too."

Lt. Bob must have known what to expect, but he didn't back down. "Listen, Diane, tell London only half the maquis in Haute Loire have weapons, but we will not wait much longer. These are prideful men filled with boldness, and they will attack to liberate Le Puy with or without the help of London. We cannot wait. Tomorrow is day nine. The maquis will attack on day ten."

He turned around and placed his hand on the doorknob but then paused, pivoted, and gave me a puzzled look. "But who are these Englishmen, Diane, these Jedburghs? Perhaps I know better, but the maquis will think the English and Americans are coming to challenge their leadership."

"The Jeds," I said, "are three-man teams—an American, a Brit and a Frenchman. They'll help direct the sabotage and bring other maquis together for future ops."

Bob nodded and opened the door to leave, but I interrupted his departure. "I have one piece of good news for you. Listen, I know we will get the drop soon, because southern France is becoming hot.

London says a second invasion is coming from the Med. Operation Dragoon. When they drive north, they'll need a strong maquis in Haute Loire to squeeze the Germans from France. That means we'll get our drop soon."

*   *   *

The next evening, the river had crested. Not five, as I had hoped, but four de Havillands from Algeria dropped their load from the sky. It was a long but good night; we lost only eight of the eighty tightly packed canisters. The Jeds' Team Jeremy, didn't arrive. Their mission had been scrubbed. The weapons and explosives were quickly divided, and the maquis made plans to depart the next day.

Before they left, Lt. Bob stopped by my house. He opened the door without knocking. "Listen, Diane. Our men are so few," Bob said. "We need to create fear and terror in the enemy. Cause them to lose reasoning and put into their minds that we have more men that can do more damage than reality says we can." He clasped his hands behind his back and looked up. "We should not slowly squeeze the enemy over time but concentrate our acts of sabotage in a single day."

I had to catch my breath. "Are you asking to change our plans? All the sabotage on just one day?" I asked with a touch of sarcasm. "We received just four aircraft, and we're still low on weapons and explosives, and you say use it up all at once?" I was speaking my thoughts. "We risk not having enough for follow-up ops. Or to defend ourselves. You know how long we waited for those flights."

"I know it is a risky move," he said. "But if we hit them quickly, create enough disarray, the enemy will think a superior army is invading, and they will flee Le Puy in panic."

"And if you are wrong?"

"Look. Our men are like angry dogs straining on a leash and will fight with vigor. Their speed and the targets they destroy will make the maquis look bigger than it is. This is not my idea alone. Hulet, Fayolle, Gevold and the rest agree. This is the best way to trick the Germans and liberate the city."

In their minds, the plan was set, and though I wasn't fully

persuaded, I trusted Bob. It was a united plan. This force of men was becoming independent, taking responsibility for their country, and I didn't argue. I let it stand.

Cuthbert and I held the job that carried the most worry: commanding the action and reporting the results back to London.

The morning of August third arrived, and by noon, couriers and radio reports began arriving from the field. I was consumed by the drama unfolding that day, thinking about Lt. Bob and how the rest of the maquis were faring—plotting the movements of troops on a map, imagining the firefights, who might be wounded or dying on the field. The early returns were encouraging, and throughout the day, I issued multiple reports to London:

- **In the south, Gevold's maquis blew the bridge at Montagnac, the Solignac tunnel and cut the N88 road.**

- **In the west, Huelot's men derailed a freight train in the tunnel at Monistrol D'Allier and blew 15 meters of track.**

- **The Brassac freight train was derailed in the tunnel railroad in the east; Fayolle demolished another railway bridge west of Le Puy.**

- **Lt. Bob's men in the north blew a railway bridge at Lavoute and another at Chamalieres, driving the locomotive into the gulf below.**

Le Puy was encircled, and its main arteries—roads, bridges, train lines, communications—all were severed just as planned. It could have been the fear of the Allies coming or the ruthless execution of our attacks that made our forces look ten feet tall. Whatever it was, the ruse worked. Panic spread within the German Army, and they ran, fearing that, now encircled, they would be trapped in Le Puy.

When the Germans fled in disarray, we were ready. Five hundred soldiers surrendered to our vastly smaller force, and five days later, August 8, 1944, the new French army joined with the maquis of the Haute Loire to liberate the regional capital. The German general staff never made it to Le Puy. And where were the Jedburghs, our Allied support? They landed, as did two other OSS men, Hemon and Rafael, after the battle, just as we were driving the remaining enemy troops from the area.

*   *   *

We were about to head out to chase the remnants of the German army from Haute Loire when one of the OSS men, the one with the codename Hemon, asked if I wanted to accompany him on a special expedition.

Hemon was an OSS weapons trainer and had a playful, whimsical attitude toward life. Laughing with the troops and irreverent toward the maquis leaders, he wasn't the least impressed with position or rank. I respected his knowledge and the way he handled himself around weapons, and I liked his self-deprecating way and his irreverence toward authority. But he was a clown, a bit frivolous, and I saw in him things that I was not. Open and funny, he had a laugh that was unhesitating and unreserved.

Hemon seemed never to be around. His job was to train men on the Sten and Browning, manual and semiautomatic, long guns, mortars, and plastic explosives. He was always blowing something up—old tree stumps, derelict equipment. And then he'd head off, wandering the woods. He had a reputation as a gourmet cook and took excursions to look for truffles or herbs for his latest creation.

That afternoon, he surprised me by asking if I'd care to join him. "My hunt for the illusive morel," he called it.

I needed a diversion and Hemon seemed to be it. He showed me where he had hidden two abandoned bicycles under the brush by the side of the road and said there was a patch of chanterelles by a rotting log on the property of an abandoned building just a mile down the road.

The bombed-out chateau was just where he said it would be. Its walls were black with soot, and the roof had collapsed. He hopped off the bicycle and without saying a word, made his way in. I was curious about what he was searching for and lagged behind.

As he kicked aside the boards of the collapsed roof and lowered himself under the beams, he seemed to know exactly where he was going. The kitchen. It was mostly destroyed, but it did have an old country cupboard that was intact. He rummaged through its contents much like a bloodhound would sniff for a bird. "Maybe there are some spices here," he called back to me. "I want to make a braised rabbit in cognac tonight."

He was joking, of course. We had neither rabbit nor brandy at the camp, but I went along with his preposterous adventure. After digging around, he came back with a little bottle, intact, with what looked like dust inside. "*Herbs de Provence*," Hemon announced proudly.

Hemon continued his exploration into a portion of the chateau that was less damaged. Before disappearing behind a door, he called out, "Now for the wine to go with our braised rabbit."

I still thought this search both ridiculous and futile. The only thing he'd find searching in all that rusty rubble would be tetanus. I waited at the top of the stairs.

Five minutes later he called up. "Diane, I think you'll be surprised if you join me downstairs."

Cuthbert and I descended slowly. There wasn't a railing, but the afternoon light through the roof made it easier for me to see my way. I met Hemon by a wine rack, inspecting his amazing find.

He looked at me in a curious way. Playful and open.

I didn't know him all that well, but I could tell he liked women, and he wanted to share what he'd found. I supposed that since I was the only woman around, he wanted to share it with me. I caught him glancing at the hem of my skirt when he thought I wasn't looking. I was sure he was curious. What was a woman dressed in matronly clothes with a wooden leg doing, fighting with the maquis? Well, those questions might surface once we began working together, but certainly not now.

"I see you have a wooden leg and yet you work with the maquis," Hemon said as he sniffed the cork of a bottle he had just opened. "It's a Chateau Lafite '25, a good vintage."

His question surprised me, but it had been offered in such a natural, open way that although I hardly knew him, I went through my story—how I got my wound hunting and how Cuthbert became my companion.

"I am disappointed," he said. "I thought your wound was achieved in battle. You must change your story when you tell it to the maquis. Now for me, the only wound I suffer is to my pride, having arrived too late to this war."

There were a couple of dusty glasses on a table beside the rack. He tugged his shirt loose and wiped them clean. "I hope this wine meets with your approval, Mademoiselle."

Really now. My hair was gray and I was in those old clothes, but still, he seemed to be flirting with me. He was funny, this Frenchman. I saw him glance at the hem of my skirt again, and though he seemed a robust man, I was quite sure his curiosity wasn't fueled by lust for a forty-year-old woman.

I had never really taken a good look at Hemon before. Yes, I'd heard the French roll smoothly off his tongue, but now I was giving him a second glance. He was a handsome man, dark with narrow, almost delicate French features, but he was a full head shorter than me and certainly younger.

Then he told me not to call him Hemon. For that evening, his name was Paul.

He'd brought his knife with him—he said there might be soldiers around, which could have been true. But I was beginning to think it all a ruse. He had brought his knife to kill the rabbit he had in a pen at the back of the chateau so that he could make dinner right there. I claimed that he had known all along about the chateau, that it wasn't a surprise—he'd equipped it with the utensils he needed to make dinner for me. He denied it, but there was a twinkle in his eye when he told me that I was crazy.

After the second bottle of Lafite, and having had my fill of braised rabbit, we moved upstairs and found a threadbare couch by a fireplace. As the fire popped and cracked, we gazed up at the stars through a hole in the ceiling. I told Paul that I had grown up on a farm. He said he was from a large family in a French immigrant community in New York City. Our conversation was so smooth, and he revealed himself so completely to me that I surprised myself by what I said. I'd never spoken of Emil—at least not since Madame Guerin had asked me years before.

And now I thought it so improbable—where we were and what might happen.

But with the pressure of war receding and the wine loosening our tongues, anything seemed possible.

EPILOGUE

---

*Working in a region infested with enemy troops, and constantly
hunted by the Gestapo, with utter disregard for her safety and
continually at the risk of capture, torture and death, she directed the
Resistance Forces with extraordinary success in acts of sabotage and
guerilla warfare against enemy troops, installations and communications. Miss Hall displayed rare courage, perseverance and ingenuity;
her efforts contributed materially to the successful operations of the
Resistance Forces in support of the Allied Expeditionary
Forces in the liberation of France.*

CITATION FOR VIRGINIA HALL
DISTINGUISHED SERVICE CROSS

In September 1944, after helping to liberate Le Puy and the Haute
Loire, Virginia was ordered back to London, where she was
to wait for her next mission. As the months passed, the Allies
continued to make gains on the battlefield, clearing France and
pushing the Nazis farther into their homeland. While the end was
in sight, it was far from the clean sweep the Americans had hoped
for. Most believed the hardest fighting would come in Germany and
Austria just before final victory. Virginia, who spoke five languages,
including German, finally was assigned another mission in April
1945: she was to head a new OSS team, part of Operation Fairmont
in Austria, where the Nazis were expected to mount a last-ditch
effort to stave off defeat.

Now possessing documents bearing the name Anna Muller and using the code name Camille, Virginia's mission was to do what she did best: organize resistance groups, conduct sabotage operations, and report intelligence information back to the Allies from her base in Innsbruck. But on the eve of her infiltration into the Austrian countryside, the news broke that the German Army was on the verge of capitulation. OSS didn't want to endanger Virginia's life needlessly. Her mission was scrubbed.

Though years had passed since her first mission in the Haute Loire, Virginia never forgot her agents. In June 1945, one month after the Allies' victory in Europe, Virginia embarked on her final assignment for the OSS. Accompanied by her companion, Hemon (his true name was Paul Goillot), Virginia traveled nearly 1,000 miles through the French countryside to find those she'd left behind.

Virginia learned that nearly all her agents had been captured and tortured by the gestapo. Dr. Rousset, the passionate medical man who had assisted wounded pilots and agents, had been the first to be apprehended, arrested as Virginia was escaping across the Pyrenees. Though he knew the details of many SOE's operations throughout France, he refused to talk under torture and was sent to the concentration camp in Buchenwald, where he saved many lives as the camp's volunteer doctor. He was liberated when the Allies overran the camp in August 1945.

Several months after Virginia's escape, Madame Guerin, the brothel owner who offered safe haven and safe houses, was arrested by the gestapo, brutally beaten, and dispatched to Ravensbruk concentration camp near Furstenburg, Germany. Guerin was one of 130,000 women in the camp. By war's end, nearly half of Ravensbruk's inmates had perished, worked to death as slave laborers or subjected to ghastly medical experimentation. Madame Germaine Guerin survived imprisonment and was liberated from the camp the spring of 1945.

Madame Catin, Virginia's courier in Le Puy, captured by the gestapo in early 1943, was beaten, tortured, and sent first to Frenes, then Ravensbruk, and finally Holleischen concentration camp in what was then Czechoslovakia. She was liberated by the Americans in 1945. Her husband fled to the mountains to fight with the maquis.

Virginia's "Vichy correspondent" and most productive agent, Suzanne Bertillon was captured by the gestapo in the spring of 1943 and sent to Moulin Prison, east of Lyon. Freed in August 1944, Bertillon later was awarded the Croix de Guerre, France's highest wartime honor, by French President Charles de Gaulle.

Virginia's talkative companion, Aramis, spent the war in Paris painting by the Seine. There's no record that the safe houses he watched around Paris were visited by the Allies.

The Abbe, whose true name was Father Robert Alesch, was responsible for the capture and death of many Allied agents. He was arrested by the gestapo and eventually released, only later to be captured by the Allies. Surviving members of the Gloria network testified at the priest's trial at the Court of Justice of the Seine, and on January 25, 1949, the 42-year-old catholic priest was executed by firing squad at Fort Montrouge prison near Paris.

Miraculously, most of those who served Virginia in the Haute Loire survived but bore the physical and mental scars of captivity, and returned to homes looted and destroyed by the Nazis. Without money or other resources, some, Virginia noted in letters to OSS leaders, were wearing clothes loaned to them or garments of sack cloth made in their concentration camps. Because Madame Guerin, Dr. Rousset, the Catins and others had been agents of the United Kingdom and the United States, France did not provide restitution, so Virginia took it upon herself to petition the US government to assist her agents. Ultimately, they received partial compensation and recognition of their honorable service.

Virginia resigned from the Office of Strategic Services, but not before receiving the Distinguished Service Cross, the second highest military award, for her bravery. She was the only civilian woman of the Second World War so honored. Still, she refused the presentation by President Truman, preferring instead the anonymity of a small ceremony in William Donovan's Office with only her mother and a photographer present. The reason, she said, was that a presidential presentation would create publicity and reveal her life as an espionage agent. She wanted to continue her clandestine work.

In December 1951, Virginia got her chance by joining the newly created Central Intelligence Agency, where she became one of the organization's first female clandestine agents. There for the next fifteen years of her professional life, she recruited covert agents and planned political and psychological operations against newly installed communist regimes in Europe, the Near East, and Africa. In 1966, ailing and with her wooden companion Cuthbert still giving her fits, she retired after reaching the agency's mandatory retirement age of sixty.

Over the objections of her mother, who thought no man was good enough for her daughter, Virginia Barbara Hall married Paul Gaston Goillot in April, 1957. For the next twenty-five years, Dindy and Paul lived on a forty-acre farm outside Barnesville, Maryland, with a garden large enough to accommodate Paul's love of cooking. Virginia raised French poodles and made cheese. Throughout the remainder of her life, Virginia remained silent about her clandestine work, even to her closest relatives.

CPSIA information can be obtained
at www.ICGtesting.com
Printed in the USA
LVHW050725020519
615762LV00002B/2/P

9 781733 541503